ESSENTIALS of
Business Ethics

Essentials Series

The Essentials Series was created for busy business advisory and corporate professionals. The books in this series were designed so that these busy professionals can quickly acquire knowledge and skills in core business areas.

Each book provides need-to-have fundamentals for those professionals who must:

- Get up to speed quickly, because they have been promoted to a new position or have broadened their responsibility scope
- Manage a new functional area
- Brush up on new developments in their area of responsibility
- Add more value to their company or clients

Other books in this series include:

For more information on any of the above titles, please visit www.wiley.com.

ESSENTIALS of Business Ethics

Creating an Organization of High Integrity and Superior Performance

Denis Collins

WILEY

John Wiley & Sons, Inc.

Copyright © 2009 by Denis Collins. All rights reserved.

Published by John Wiley & Sons, Inc., Hoboken, New Jersey.
Published simultaneously in Canada.

For general information on our other products and services, or technical support, please contact our Customer Care Department within the United States at 800-762-2974, outside the United States at 317-572-3993 or fax 317-572-4002.

Wiley also publishes its books in a variety of electronic formats. Some content that appears in print may not be available in electronic books.

For more information about Wiley products, visit our Web site at www.wiley.com.

Library of Congress Cataloging-in-Publication Data

Collins, Denis, 1956-
   Essentials of business ethics: creating an organization of high integrity and superior performance/Denis Collins.
      p.   cm. – (Essentials series)
   Includes index.
   ISBN 978-0-470-44256-2 (pbk.)
   1. Business ethics.   I. Title.
   HF5387.C625 2009
   174'.4–dc22   2008054163

Printed in the United States of America

10 9 8 7 6 5 4 3 2 1

This book is dedicated to all employees creating ethical organizations.

Contents

Contents

Contents

Contents

Contents

Foreword

R alph Waldo Emerson wrote that "Life is the sum of your choices."

While Emerson was reflecting on one's personal choices, his thinking is clearly applicable to daily business decisions. A leader's most important responsibility is to establish the ethical culture of the organization—that is, the values that underlie the behavior of *all* employees, partners, and other stakeholders.

Corporations may espouse laudable corporate values, such as quality, integrity, and community, but these all spring from ethics—essentially, knowing the difference between right and wrong. Values are what you believe, what you say, and what you do. If key stakeholders—customers and employees—perceive cognitive dissonance between those elements, then the leader needs to re-evaluate his or her thinking and actions to avoid disloyalty, mediocre performance, and high turnover. The strong, effective leader will accept that he or she is vulnerable to the possibility of making a mistake—a poor decision—and be prepared to take appropriate, swift corrective action. The effective leader is not so arrogant as to shirk accountability.

One of the most difficult challenges for an organization is to recruit individuals who demonstrate and sustain ethical behavior over time. At Physicians Plus Insurance, ethical behavior was a clear *core competency* required in all executive and management job descriptions, and was part of the annual performance review. The perception of ethical leadership has been measured annually for several years through an all-employee Great Place to Work® survey. The practice of ethical behavior is essential to high performance and long-term, competitive sustainability.

The topic of ethics is a difficult subject for leaders that is easily side-stepped, as it is human nature to avoid complex issues. Ethics is not a required course in most graduate business curricula. Emphasis is given to the "hard" business sciences, such as accounting, finance, marketing, information technology, operations management, and so on. But, in fact, ethics *is* the hardest subject to understand and it may take a lifetime of thought, concentration, and practice to master. It's ironic that ethics is not the first prerequisite of business school programs nor consciously integrated into every course in the curriculum. As a precondition of graduation, students should write and defend a major paper on the topic of ethical leadership.

The most ethical enterprises practice transparency and fairness in decision-making; open, two-way communication between leaders and stakeholders; and accountability to stakeholders (customers, taxpayers, patients, congregates) who *trust* their leaders to do the right thing. The business leader's most important job is to establish the organization's ethical boundaries, convey clear and explicit expectations of the leadership team, and teach these principles to all employees, so that ethical thinking becomes part of the organization's genetic code.

I presented the core values of Physicians Plus Insurance, embodied in our Code of Ethics, at new employee orientations. I made it clear that ethics is a matter of trust: If we lost the trust of our customers because of perceived ethical breaches, we would be out of business. Being an insurance company, adherence to this code could be a competitive advantage.

All employees were required to attend our annual ethics conference, and all managers received mandatory ethics training. Frequently, I would author an article in the employee newsletter addressing the topic of ethics, using real examples pertinent to our business. The Board of Directors, which has ultimate responsibility for an organization's adherence to ethical standards, also grappled with an ethical dilemma as part of its regular Board agenda—sometimes it was hypothetical, but sometimes it was real.

The failure of ethical leadership in an organization is very destructive; it demoralizes the workforce, breeds public distrust, and ultimately results in organizational decay. Think about the legacy that you want to leave: Do you want to be remembered as a ruthless and heartless person who despoiled the value of the business entrusted to you, or as a leader who, through the daily application of ethical leadership principles, created value for stakeholders, including inspiring your employees to join you in leaving the world a better place?

In his previous book, *Behaving Badly: Ethical Lessons from Enron*, Professor Denis Collins observed that "ethical perfection is a goal that is always a few steps into the future, where it remains our entire lives." By applying the wealth of practical advice in his latest book, you will be taking a giant step forward.

Martin A. Preizler
President, MPAworldclass
(www.MPAworldclass.com)
Former President and CEO,
Physicians Plus Health Insurance Corporation

Preface

A business is a community of individuals that transforms resources obtained from suppliers into products and services customers find useful. The same is true for nonprofit organizations and local, state, and federal government agencies. Their scorecards differ—a balanced budget instead of profits—but their activities are similar. Sufficient revenue must be generated, or activities will come to a halt.

Organizations of high integrity achieve superior performance because they attract and retain high-quality employees, customers, suppliers, and investors. Creating organizations of high integrity takes time and effort; it does not happen automatically, because human beings are not morally perfect. Unethical employees, customers, suppliers, and investors can prevent organizations from achieving high integrity and superior performance. In addition, unethical organizations can be profitable . . . in the short term, not the long term.

So how do you create an ethical organization? This book, which is based on more than two decades of consulting, teaching, and researching, contains all the things I would do if I were the CEO.

General Overview

Chapter 1: Human Nature and Unethical Behavior in Organizations. Managers must recognize that moral imperfection is a fact of life, and then develop systems and checks-and-balances to minimize the exercise of moral imperfections within their own organization. This chapter discusses research and insights on human nature, and its implications at the workplace.

Chapter 2: The Ethical Foundation of Capitalism and the Optimal Ethics Systems Model. People engaged in business activities have been acting ethically and unethically since the beginning of human history. This chapter describes the ethical basis of capitalism and the Federal Sentencing Guidelines. An Optimal Ethics Systems Model is proposed as a framework for maximizing ethical behaviors in organizations.

Chapter 3: Hiring Ethical People. Hiring just one employee with an unethical value system—someone whose sense of morality and justice does not match that of a high-integrity work culture—can corrupt an organization. This chapter reviews the current research on a variety of ethics-related job screening techniques, such as background checks and integrity tests, to determine which methods are more likely to differentiate between ethical and unethical job candidates. A five-step process for evaluating the ethics of job candidates is developed.

Chapter 4: Codes of Ethics and Codes of Conduct. Ethical dilemmas arise because people have different ethical beliefs, and many situations are ambiguous. An organization's Code of Ethics serves as its conscience and provides employees with a common ethical reference point. This chapter explains the differences between a Code of Ethics and a Code of Conduct, summarizes their prevalence and content, and describes how to use a Code of Ethics to assess and improve ethical performance.

Chapter 5: Ethical Decision-Making Framework. Employees need to know how to independently derive a moral answer to business issues. This chapter offers a systematic six-question ethics decision-making framework grounded in moral philosophy.

Chapter 6: Ethics Training. Ethics training initiates dialogue at work around contentious issues and helps to create a culture of trust. This chapter describes ten different types of ethics training workshops that have received very favorable responses from managers and employees.

Chapter 7: Respecting Employee Diversity. The population of the United States continues to diversify, as does the employee and customer base of organizations. This chapter describes the competitive advantages of a diverse workforce, offers a 10-step process for implementing a diversity initiative, describes best practices for managing diversity, and provides several diversity training exercises.

Chapter 8: Ethics Reporting Systems. Managers must be made aware of, and employees need to discuss, ethical issues as they arise. This chapter describes how to manage three internal communication mechanisms for employees to report potential unethical or illegal behaviors: an Ethics & Compliance Officer, an Ombudsman, and Ethics Hotlines. A failure in these internal communication systems can result in external whistleblowing, which is damaging for both the organization and the whistleblower.

Chapter 9: Ethical Leadership, Work Goals, and Performance Appraisals. Three aspects of daily organizational life significantly impact an employee's ethical performance: the direct supervisor's behaviors, work goals, and performance appraisals. This chapter describes how managers are ethical role models, how to use Management-By-Objectives to establish work goals that encourage ethical behavior, and how to create performance appraisals that reward ethical behaviors.

Chapter 10: Empowering Ethical Employees. Managers should develop workplaces where employees are empowered to be in control of their immediate surroundings and have the freedom and authority to do what needs to get done. This chapter explores how to create effective problem-solving teams, use the Appreciative Inquiry technique to develop plans for superior customer service, implement a Scanlon-type gainsharing plan and Open Book Management, and distribute financial improvements to all employees through profit sharing, stock options, employee stock ownership plans, and cooperatives.

Chapter 11: Environmental Management. Many managers now realize that appropriately managing the relationship between organizational operations and the environment can enhance profits and long-term success. This chapter examines how to manage the environmental change process, create an Environmental Management System, identify environmental risks, develop measurable environmental goals and objectives, and assess environmental performance.

Chapter 12: Community Outreach and Respect. The well-being of the host community profoundly impacts an organization, and vice versa. This chapter describes how to develop a diverse portfolio of giving opportunities, align community outreach with the company's mission and assets, choose a strategic partner, administer the community involvement process, and assess and report social performance.

Each chapter in this book also contains an *In the Real World* scenario based on a tragic organizational experience: Enron. Enron's sudden collapse in December 2001 was not inevitable, nor did it happen overnight. At any point between 1985 and 2001, Enron's misdirected evolution could have been corrected through different aspects of the Optimal Ethics Systems Model. Thirteen key decisions are presented in chronological order from several perspectives, including those of Ken Lay, Jeff Skilling, accountants, and investment bankers. Readers are challenged to decide what they would have done if employed by, or doing business with, Enron.

This book is a managerial "how-to" manual that can be implemented immediately. Do not hesitate to contact me at dcollins@ edgewood.edu if you wish to discuss any of the recommendations. We need each other's assistance in creating organizations of high integrity and superior performance.

I am a terminal cancer survivor, thirteen years and counting, and there is no better way to spend time on Earth than to help create ethical organizations and an ethical society.

Denis Collins
April 2009

About the Web Site

As a purchaser of this book, *Essentials of Business Ethics: Creating an Organization of High Integrity and Superior Performance*, you have access to the supporting Web site:

www.wiley.com/go/businessethics

This Web site contains a 76 item best practices survey.

The password to enter this site is: ethics

Acknowledgments

I would like to thank my Edgewood College colleagues for taking on the challenge of teaching about business ethics across the Business School curriculum.

I am indebted to Sheck Cho for suggesting that I write this book and to Stacey Rivera, Darcie Moore, and Natasha Andrews-Noel for their careful editing and managing of the material. I also thank Dianne Jenkins, Seth Collins, Anna Collins, Connor, Milo, Lisa Goldthorpe, and Beth Tryon for contributing ideas or providing general assistance in the writing of this book.

Lastly, I offer a special thanks to students, workshop participants, and clients for accepting the challenge to implement the best practices discussed in this book.

PART 1

Background

CHAPTER 1

Human Nature and Unethical Behavior in Organizations

After reading this chapter, you will be able to:

- Explain the competitive advantages of creating and maintaining an ethical organization
- Describe some common types of unethical behaviors that occur in all types of organizations—for-profits, nonprofits, educational institutions, and government
- Appreciate that unethical behaviors can occur in all organizational operations
- Understand that unethical behaviors can be very costly to organizations
- Discuss human nature in terms of people being pleasure-seekers who can choose to do good or bad

Businesses, nonprofit organizations, and government agencies significantly improve the quality of life on Earth by providing goods and services that fulfill consumer needs.

Look around. A business built the house you live in, the alarm clock that wakes you up, the bed you sleep in, the clothes you wear, the newspapers you read, the chair you sit in, the food you eat, the music you listen to, and the car you drive to work. Providing goods and services that enrich the quality of life, and employment, are very ethical endeavors.

Ethics should permeate all aspects of organizational operations. Unfortunately, due to human nature and inappropriate management control systems, many organizations are ethically challenged.

This chapter discusses why managing ethics is essential, moral imperfection among human beings, and the nature and negative ramifications of unethical activities within organizations. Almost every decision made every day has ethical ramifications. Managing ethics appropriately leads to superior financial performance.

Daily Occurrence of Ethical Dilemmas

When an organization employs someone, that individual brings to work not only unique job skills, but also his or her ethics. Ethics is the set of principles a person uses to determine whether an action is good or bad. Ethics permeates every stakeholder interaction involving owners, customers, employees, lenders, suppliers, and government officials.

People experience a multitude of ethical dilemmas on a daily basis, beginning with whether to get out of bed or hit the snooze button when the morning alarm goes off. Almost every decision and action a person makes the rest of the day has an impact on other people, beginning with arriving at work on time and ending with unfinished tasks at the end of the day. Each decision and action is subject to ethical analysis.

An action sequence consists of the motivation behind the act, the act itself, and the consequences of the act. An ideal ethical situation is one in which a person has good motives and the act results in good consequences. The most unethical situation is one where a person has bad motives and the act results in bad consequences.

Is it ethical for you to inform a subordinate about next year's business plan? It depends. If you have permission to share the information and doing so improves the subordinate's performance, then it is very ethical. However, if sharing the information violates a confidentiality agreement and the subordinate is likely to misuse the information, then it is very unethical.

On the ethics continuum, some situations fall between the two extremes. Sometimes, good motives can generate bad consequences. For instance, trying to help a colleague perform one task might distract the person from meeting an important deadline. Sometimes, bad motives can generate good consequences. Your selfish refusal to support a colleague in need of assistance may result in the colleague obtaining even better support from someone else. When evaluating these less-than-ethically-ideal situations, some people place greater ethical weight on having proper motives, while others place greater weight on achieving favorable consequences.

Without having been trained in philosophy, few managers realize that almost every business decision has ethical ramifications. For instance, in 1985, Ken Lay, chief executive officer (CEO) of the regional Houston Natural Gas (HNG) company, had to decide whether to accept a merger offer from InterNorth, which owned North America's largest natural gas pipeline (see *In the Real World*). The ethical implications of this business decision are profound. Lay's decision would impact all InterNorth and HNG shareholders, all HNG employees and their families, and the cities of Houston, Texas and Omaha, Nebraska.

IN THE REAL WORLD

Merger Opportunity—1985

In 1985, corporate raider Irwin "The Liquidator" Jacobs proposed a hostile takeover of the financially troubled InterNorth, an Omaha, Nebraska firm that operated the largest national gas pipeline in North America. InterNorth's CEO contacted Ken Lay, the CEO of a regional company called Houston Natural Gas (HNG), about a potential merger. InterNorth proposed purchasing HNG's $47 stock at $70 a share, for a total price tag of $2.4 billion, much of it borrowed money. Jacob's hostile takeover of InterNorth would be prevented because, even if he sold all the newly combined company's corporate assets, Jacobs could not profitably pay off its huge debt.

The merger proposal made strategic sense for the regional HNG. The federal government was in the process of deregulating the energy industry and the combined entity would be a dominant force in the natural gas market. In addition, Lay and other executives could sell their HNG stock options at the premium price being offered by InterNorth.

But there were some potential negative merger ramifications for Lay to consider. The InterNorth/HNG entity would have to manage a daunting $4.3 billion debt. Also, it would be a merger of unequal partners. InterNorth, with $7.5 billion in revenue, was three times larger than HNG. Such a size disparity typically resulted in the smaller firm being taken over by the larger one. Bureaucratic redundancies would be eliminated to achieve cost reductions. Only one CEO would be needed, not two, and corporate control would transfer from Houston to Omaha.

DECISION CHOICE. If you were the CEO of HNG, would you:

 Reject InterNorth's proposal to protect your job and keep HNG headquartered in Houston?

❷ Merge with North America's largest natural gas pipeline company, although it meant the risk of managing a large debt, relocating corporate headquarters to Nebraska, and losing jobs due to redundancies?

Why?

Competitive Advantages of Ethical Organizations

Ethical organizations consist of ethical employees empowered to operate within a culture of trust. Research findings (and common sense) strongly suggest that, in the long term, ethical organizations financially outperform unethical organizations. Eight competitive advantages of achieving high integrity within a culture of trust appear in Exhibit 1.1.

If you were a *job applicant*, would you rather work for an ethical or an unethical organization?

An ethical organization attracts high-quality employees and leads to higher levels of employee satisfaction and loyalty. If the pay is similar, job candidates consistently choose the ethical organization rather than the unethical organization. Individuals only choose the

EXHIBIT 1.1

Competitive Advantages of Being Ethical and Trustworthy

Ethical organizations, compared to unethical organizations:

1. Attract and retain higher quality employees
2. Attract and retain higher quality customers
3. Attract and retain higher quality suppliers
4. Attract and retain higher quality investors
5. Earn goodwill with community members and government officials
6. Achieve greater efficiency and decision making, based on more reliable information from stakeholders
7. Achieve higher product quality
8. Need less employee supervision

unethical organization if pay and benefits are substantially higher. A survey of MBA students found that 94% of them would accept an average of 14% lower pay to work for an organization with a reputation for high ethical standards.[1]

If you were a *customer*, would you rather purchase products or services from an ethical or unethical organization?

A stellar ethical reputation is priceless marketing and leads to higher levels of customer satisfaction and loyalty. When product price and quality are similar, potential customers consistently choose the ethical organization over the unethical organization. In fact, consumers are willing to pay a modest premium for products and services supplied by an ethical company. They purchase from an unethical organization only if the price is substantially lower.

If you were a *supplier*, would you rather sell your products and services to an ethical or unethical organization?

An ethical organization attracts high-quality suppliers and increases supplier satisfaction and loyalty. Potential suppliers consistently choose to sell to the ethical organization that pays a fair price rather than the unethical organization. Suppliers depend on customers to pay their bills on time so that they can manage a smooth operation.

If you were an *investor*, would you rather do business with an ethical or unethical organization?

High-quality investors are attracted to ethical organizations, which leads to higher levels of investor satisfaction and loyalty. If anticipated return-on-investments are similar, potential lenders and investors consistently choose the ethical organization rather than the unethical organization.

If you were a *community leader* or *government official*, would you rather interact with an ethical or unethical organization?

Ethical organizations honestly communicate with stakeholders and pay their fair share of taxes. In return, ethical organizations earn the respect of, and gain access to, community leaders and government officials.

Lastly, if you were an employee, customer, supplier, investor, community leader, or government official, would you provide managers of an ethical organization with truthful or deceptive information?

We tend to treat others as they treat us. People who are treated fairly and truthfully tend to reply in a fair and truthful manner.

Managers can make better informed decisions when they know that the information supplied by others is trustworthy. The honest flow of ideas and the higher levels of employee loyalty, commitment, and satisfaction result in better quality consumer products and services and reduce the need for employee supervision.

These common sentiments are supported by survey research reported in 2007:[2]

- 94% of Americans believe it is "critical" or "important" to work for an ethical company.

- 33% of employees have left a company because they disagreed with its business ethics.

- 70% of Americans have decided not to purchase a company's product because of its questionable ethics.

- 72% of Americans prefer to buy higher priced products and services from companies with ethical business practices than lower priced products and services from companies with questionable business practices.

TIPS AND TECHNIQUES

Persuading Employees of the Importance of Being Ethical

Being ethical is the right thing to do, but telling that to someone who is not concerned about ethics, or is considering an unethical act, will likely fall on deaf ears. Instead, build a business case linking ethical behavior to profitability or other financial impacts. That usually gets the person's attention.

Begin by developing a list of reasons why being ethical is good for your organization's bottom line. Compelling reasons typically include customer retention, lower costs, higher product quality, and employee morale.

Managing Morally Imperfect People

Organizations are composed of people. The average human being is a very good person. But he or she is not a saint. Everyone has his or her own set of moral challenges to manage, such as greed, anger, envy, lust, and pride. Moral perfection is a moving target, always a few grasps beyond our reach.

The managerial challenge is to coordinate the transformation of inputs into products and services in a way that respects the dignity of owners, employees, customers, suppliers, the host community, and the natural environment. It only takes one unethical or illegal behavior to ruin an organization's reputation or result in damaging litigation.

Researchers have documented that the average person lies twice a day. That's actually pretty good when one considers the thousands of statements the average person makes every day. But those two times a day an employee, customer, or supplier are dishonest can be very problematic for organizations.

The dishonesty could be a big lie (e.g., a manager falsely claims that the organization has surpassed revenue targets) or a small one (e.g., a salesperson falsely tells an aggravated customer that the boss is not in the office today). The dishonesty could be a lie of commission (e.g., falsely telling the boss that the work is complete) or one of omission (e.g., not telling the boss anything about the incomplete work).

Due to human nature and the potential negative ramifications of unethical work-related activities on organizational performance, ethics must be managed.

What is the Extent of Unethical Behaviors at Work?

Although people are good most of the time, researchers report a rather high prevalence of unethical behavior at work:

- 67% of chief financial officers (CFOs) have been pressured to misrepresent corporate results.[3]

- 25% of middle managers have written a fraudulent internal report.[4]

- 75% of employees have stolen at least once from their employer.[5]

- 33% of employees calling in sick are really tending to personal needs or feel entitled to a day off.[6]

The Ethics Resource Center surveyed more than 3,000 employees in 2005 about ethical issues at work.[7] Of the respondents, 52% observed at least one type of misconduct in the workplace during the past year. Only 55% of these were reported to management; 48% of the misconducts violated the law.

The most common types of misconduct employees observed were abusive or intimidating behavior towards employees, lying, employees placing their own interests over organizational interests, safety violations, misreporting of actual time worked, illegal discrimination, and stealing.

As for our future business leaders, 56% of MBAs admit to cheating on a class assignment during the previous academic year.[8]

What Types of Organizations and Operational Areas Have Ethical Problems?

Ethical issues arise in every organization and throughout organizational operations.

Unethical discrimination based on race or gender can occur in dealings with suppliers, employees, customers, the government, or the public. They could occur in any department—accounting, finance, human resources, or marketing. They could occur at any level of the organization—Board of Directors, executives, middle managers, staff, or production employees. They could be engrained in an organization's job recruitment practices, job screening practices, terms of employment, job tasks, training opportunities, performance evaluations, or layoffs.

Ethical problems can arise in any organization, even the most admirable ones. Xerox has won many awards for their excellent diversity programs. Despite these efforts, Xerox was fined $12 million in 2008 for racial discrimination.[9]

Why Do Good People Behave Unethically?

Ethics would be easy to manage if simply a matter of detecting and dismissing evil people. But that is not the nature of organizational life.

Sometimes the unethical decision or outcome is not intentional. Unethical situations can arise when a good person has insufficient knowledge and awareness, inadequate job skills, or lacks prudence, judgment, or courage.[10] Ethical problems also result from management and organizational design issues, such as a misaligned management system, inadequate flow of information, perceived management indifference, inadequate legal and regulatory framework, and pressures from unethical customers or competitors.

Sometimes good people will occasionally behave unethically because of contextual reasons. A survey conducted by the Society for Human Resource Management and the Ethics Resource Center found that 24% of the respondents were pressured to compromise ethical standards either periodically, fairly often, or all the time. Of those feeling pressured, the top five organizational sources were:[11]

1. Following the boss's directives (experienced by 49%)

2. Meeting overly aggressive business or financial objectives (48%)

3. Helping the organization to survive (40%)

4. Meeting schedule pressures (35%)

5. Wanting to be a team player (27%)

What are the Costs of Unethical Behaviors?

Unethical behaviors can be very costly. The Equal Employment Opportunity Commission (EEOC) maintains an annual database of charges filed and resolved under various antidiscrimination laws, such as age discrimination or sexual harassment.[12]

EXHIBIT 1.2

EEOC Charges and Resolutions, 1997 and 2007

Type of Discrimination	Fiscal Year 1997 Number Cases Filed	Fiscal Year 2007 Number Cases Filed	Number Cases Resolved	Monetary Benefits Determined by EEOC (excludes other forms of litigation)
Race	29,199	30,510	25,882	$67.7 million
Retaliation on all EEOC-enforced statues	Not Available	26,663	22,265	$124 million
Gender	24,728	24,826	21,982	$135.4 million
Age	15,785	19,103	16,134	$66.8 million
Disability	18,108	17,734	15,708	$677 million
Sexual harassment	15,889	12,510	11,592	$49.9 million
National origin	6,712	9,396	7,773	$22.8 million
Pregnancy	3,977	5,587	4,979	$30 million
Religion	1,709	2,880	2,525	$6.4 million
Equal pay and compensation	1,134	818	796	$9.3 million

Exhibit 1.2 summarizes the totals for fiscal year 2007 and offers a comparison to fiscal year 1997. The discriminations are listed in order of the number of cases filed in 2007, with 30,510 racial discrimination filings leading the pack, followed closely by retaliation

filings. This represents only a portion of all alleged cases of workplace discriminations, as many go unreported.

What is Human Nature?

The survey results and costly penalties associated with all types of organizations beg the question: Are human beings born good or bad?

According to social philosophers, human beings are born neither good nor bad. Psychologically, human beings are born with a desire to experience happiness. Babies exhibit a natural tendency to pursue their own self-interests, which entails doing things that generate pleasure and avoiding things that generate pain. This tendency, supplemented by a concern for the well-being of others, continues throughout our lives.

Some of the ways we pursue pleasure are very ethical, such as being honest and helping others. Other methods are unethical, such as lying to avoid punishment. Among young children, behaviors praised by parents are considered good and those criticized by parents are considered bad. Being yelled at, or ostracized, causes psychological pain, which children then try to avoid.

As children age into adulthood, other moral influences include siblings, friends, media, teachers, religious authorities, colleagues, and the boss. Sometimes these multiple perspectives are in harmony, other times in conflict. When moral perspectives conflict in a meaningful situation, people apply reason to determine the right thing to do. Different people reach different moral conclusions. The end result can be an individual like Bill Gates donating his business fortune to solve social problems, or someone like Jeff Skilling leading Enron into unethical oblivion.

Summary

Human beings have a dual nature. We are primarily honest, but we also lie. We primarily care for our own welfare, but we also care about the welfare of others. We are kind to others, but we can also be cruel. Each person has his or her unique set of moral challenges. Everyone experiences moral successes and failures.

In the 1700s, Adam Smith conceptualized capitalism as an economic system morally superior to previous forms of economic arrangements, particularly highly regulated mercantilism. He argued that the wealth of a nation would be significantly enhanced if morally imperfect people were provided the freedom to pursue their own economic self-interests within a system of justice.

Chapter 2 explores the historical need for capitalism, and modifications made to, and within, the capitalist system to improve business ethics.

Notes

1. David Montgomery and Catherine A. Ramus, "Corporate Social Responsibility: Reputation Effects on MBA Job Choice," in G. Papanikos and C. Veloutsou (Eds.), *Global Issues of Business*, Vol. 2, Athens Institute for Education and Research (2003): 289–298.

2. *Directors & Boards* (February 2007), http://directorsandboards.com/DBEBRIEFING/February2007/bonusfeature207.html, accessed 8/29/08.

3. Advertising Supplement, *Business Week*, July 13, 1998.

4. Joseph L. Badaracco and Allen Webb, "Business Ethics: The View from the Trenches," *California Management Review*, 37, no. 2 (1995): 8–28.

5. 2004 U.S. Chamber of Commerce survey, reported at www.fvldlaw.com/newsletters/2004-02.htm, accessed 8/28/08.

6. Sue Shellenbarger, "From Pilfering Pens to Padding Expense Accounts—We're Lying More at Work," *Wall Street Journal*, March 24, 2005.

7. www.ethics.org/erc-publications/books.asp, accessed 12/18/08.

8. Donald L. McCabe, Kenneth D. Butterfield, and Linda K. Trevino, "Academic Dishonesty in Graduate Business Programs: Prevalence, Causes, and Proposed Action," *Academy of Management Learning & Education*, 5, no. 3 (2006): 294–306.

9. Kathryn A. Canas and Harris Sondak, *Opportunities and Challenges of Workplace Diversity* (Upper Saddle River, NJ: Pearson Prentice Hall, 2008): 3–4.

10. Lynn Sharp Paine, *Leadership, Ethics, and Organizational Integrity* (New York: Irwin, 1997).

11. Anonymous, "How to Help Reinvigorate Your Organization's Ethics Program," *HR Focus*, June 2003: 7–8.

12. www.eeoc.gov/types/index.html, accessed 8/28/08.

CHAPTER 2

The Ethical Foundation of Capitalism and the Optimal Ethics Systems Model

After reading this chapter, you will be able to:

- Appreciate that the best way to ensure free market capitalism is for business owners and managers to behave ethically
- Understand the ethical foundation of capitalism as argued by Adam Smith in the 1700s
- Benchmark your organization to the Ethics Compliance Program best practices outlined by the Federal Sentencing Guidelines
- Use an Optimal Ethics Systems Model to maximize ethical behaviors within your organization

People engaged in business activities have been acting ethically and unethically since the beginning of human history.

Free-market capitalism is a significant ethical improvement over previous forms of economic arrangements. People, although morally imperfect, have the freedom to pursue their own economic interests. Consumer needs are met and national wealth increased. Government laws and regulations are usually a response to business owners and managers abusing their freedom and demonstrating a lack of concern for the well-being of their employees and community.

This chapter describes the ethical foundation of capitalism developed by Adam Smith in the 1700s. The Federal Sentencing Guidelines, implemented in 1991, encourage organizations to adopt some of the best practices in business ethics. The chapter concludes with an Optimal Ethics Systems Model, based on best practices in business ethics, which maximizes ethical behavior in organizations and minimizes unethical behaviors. Each unit in the model serves as the basis for Chapters 3 through 12.

Adam Smith's Capitalism and Business Ethics

Unethical business practices such as theft from competitors, lies to consumers, and harsh working conditions appear in the earliest written histories. Governments, responsible for maintaining communal peace, have often created laws regulating what they consider to be the most unethical activities in the economic sector.

In the 1600s, mercantilism was the dominant economic system in the British Empire. Government strictly regulated product and labor markets. Adam Smith (1723-1790), a Scottish philosophy professor, formulated capitalism as an economic system ethically superior to mercantilism. Living conditions for peasants in Scotland were harsh at the time of Smith's philosophizing, and freedom was stifled. The famines of 1696-1699 and 1739-1740 resulted in the starvation of 5–10% of the Scottish population.

Smith recommended that government abandon its mercantilist policy of sanctioning monopolies, putting quotas on imports, regulating tradesmen, and restricting other aspects of economic behavior. He lashed out at the "wretched spirit of monopoly." Lack of competition under mercantilism led to high prices, shortages, and low-quality products. Key business management positions were filled based on family connections rather than individual merit.

Smith insisted that both product markets and labor markets be based on freedom and individual competition rather than government regulation. Individuals should be free to do what comes naturally—pursuing their self-interests. When this happens, producers and laborers flock to markets where demand is high and supply is low—which is where they are needed the most.

In the Real World: Skilling's Innovative Gas Bank Idea—1990 provides a modern example of this phenomenon. Should Enron continue to fight it out in a highly contested market or create a new Gas Bank Division that could dramatically impact other divisions in the company and change the natural gas market?

Trained in Protestant theology, which emphasizes human sinfulness, Smith was well aware that merchants might misuse their freedom and take advantage of customers or laborers. He maintained

Skilling's Innovative
Gas Bank Idea—1990

Ken Lay accepted InterNorth's merger proposal. Following six months of astute political maneuvering, Lay became CEO, renamed the company Enron, and kept its headquarters in Houston.

In 1986, Enron reported $14 million in losses. The $4.3 billion debt nearly bankrupted Enron in 1987, and credit-rating agencies downgraded Enron's bonds to "junk" status. Lay hired McKinsey and Company, the world's most prestigious consulting firm, to develop innovative ideas for generating desperately needed revenue. One of the consultants, Jeff Skilling, proposed that Enron create a new type of business called a Gas Bank.

The natural gas market consisted of public utilities signing short-term contracts, due to unpredictable price fluctuations, with natural gas suppliers. These short-term contracts made it impossible for either customers or suppliers to perform reliable long-term budgetary planning.

Skilling proposed a radically new business model. Enron could purchase natural gas from other suppliers by offering them long-term contracts at a premium price, and then sell the natural gas to customers by offering them long-term contracts at a premium price. This would be appealing because both suppliers and customers would have predictable long-term cash flows.

However, the Gas Bank would need a tremendous amount of capital investment, something Enron did not have, to start purchasing natural gas from competitors. Many long-time Enron managers opposed Skilling's proposal, preferring that all new investments be directed toward traditional business operations, such as drilling for new sources of natural gas.

DECISION CHOICE. If you were the CEO of Enron, would you:

1 Stay focused on what Enron already excels in, distributing natural gas through its own pipelines, and continue to search for more traditional solutions to Enron's growing debt problems?

2 Make a huge investment in creating a Gas Bank, a very risky financial endeavor never undertaken before?

Why?

that, although there would be infinite opportunities to act immorally in a free market system, most of the time individuals would choose to act morally.

Smith differentiated between selfishness (concern about oneself, without any concern about the well-being of others) and self-interest (concern about oneself in relationship to the well-being of others), and concluded that human beings were driven by self-interest, not selfishness. Although people might be tempted to behave selfishly, Smith thought, they self-regulated themselves based on moral sentiments. These moral sentiments originate from one's conscience, belief in God, and natural concern for the well-being of others. Even unethical bullies can be persuaded by reason. When these self-regulating moral mechanisms failed, a system of justice funded by, but independent of, government must punish the wrongdoer to protect the public from egregious immoral actions.

Smith's ethical defense of capitalism rests on the following beliefs:

- Freedom and liberty are essential values.

- A free people naturally pursue their own self-interests.

- People will choose to enter product and labor markets where there is the greatest need and opportunity.

- People morally self-regulate their actions based on their conscience, belief in God, concern for the well-being of others, and reason.

- A strong system of justice is essential to punish those who do not appropriately self-regulate themselves.

Federal Sentencing Guidelines

The continued existence of free-market capitalism depends on organizational employees behaving ethically. The more that organizational employees behave ethically, the more freedom managers and other employees can be granted. The more that organizational employees behave unethically, the more organizational decisions must be regulated to protect stakeholders.

In 1991, President George H.W. Bush issued new Federal Sentencing Guidelines with the intention of encouraging, though not requiring, managers to implement ethical best practices. The Federal Sentencing Guidelines are applicable to nonprofits, unions, partnerships, trusts, and universities as well as businesses.

Experts developed a list of best practices for Ethics Compliance Programs which, if implemented, significantly reduced the likelihood of unethical or criminal activity. The 16 best practices for an Ethics Compliance Program suggested by the Federal Sentencing Guidelines, divided into 6 categories, appear in Exhibit 2.1.[1] The last column provides the reader with an opportunity to benchmark his or her own organization to these best practices.

Guided by the principles of free-market economics, the government wants managers to decide which, if any, of the best practices

EXHIBIT 2.1

Best practices for ethics compliance programs

Category	Best Practice	Done!
Organizational Personnel Issue	Substantial authority is not given to any employee known to have engaged in illegal activities.	
Ethics Compliance Program Personnel	A specific high-level manager oversees the program.	
	A specific individual is accountable for the program's day-to-day operations.	
Content of the Ethics Compliance Program	Code of Ethics is developed and publicized. Procedures are established for preventing and detecting criminal misconduct or unethical behavior.	
	Mechanisms are available for employees to anonymously or confidentially seek guidance on, or report, criminal or unethical conduct without fear of retaliation.	
Management of the Ethics Compliance Program	Program training is provided to all employees. Program content is communicated throughout the organization.	

(Continued)

EXHIBIT 2.1

	(Continued)	
Category	**Best Practice**	**Done!**
	Criminal risks common to the profession or industry are periodically assessed. Program's effectiveness is periodically assessed.	
Rewards and Punishments	Employees are provided with incentives for performing in accordance with the program's provisions.	
	Incentives for ethical behavior and legal compliance are consistently enforced.	
	Employees violating the program's provisions, or who fail to take reasonable steps to prevent or detect criminal activity, are disciplined.	
	Disciplinary measures for unethical behavior or criminal misconduct are consistently enforced.	
After Criminal Conduct Detected	Reasonable steps are taken to respond appropriately to the criminal conduct.	
	Reasonable steps are taken to prevent similar criminal misconduct in the future.	
Number of Best Practices		

to implement rather than impose a one-size-fits-all approach. An organization that behaves ethically without any of the best practices could continue to operate as it has in the past. But if an employee commits a crime, the judge must determine how much the organization should be punished for the employee's criminal behavior. The judge refers to a standardized chart listing fines for specific types of crime and organizational size, and then adjusts the fine by a culpability multiplier of 0.05 to 4.0 based on the extent to which the organization has implemented the best practices.

Assume an employee commits a consumer fraud, and the corresponding fine listed in the chart is $1.2 million. If an organization has not implemented any of the best practices, the initial $1.2 million fine can be assessed a culpability multiplier of 4.0, increasing the fine to $4.8 million. The organization is being punished for not exhibiting a good-faith effort at minimizing unethical behaviors.

If, on the other hand, the organization has exhibited a good faith effort to minimize unethical behaviors by implementing the best practices, the initial $1.2 million fine could be assessed a culpability multiplier of 0.05, reducing the fine to $60,000. If some, but not all, of the best practices have been implemented, the fine will be between these two amounts.

An organization is rewarded, meaning the fine is reduced, if it has a history of behaving ethically, has implemented an effective Ethics Compliance Program, and immediately takes full responsibility for the employee's criminal activity. An organization is considered very culpable for the employee's criminal activity if it has a history of criminal activity, there is no Ethics Compliance Program, and it obstructs the government's investigation.

The Optimal Ethics Systems Model

Successful long-term organizational growth requires honesty, trust, integrity, and credibility, among other ethical values. Creating and sustaining a culture of trust for morally imperfect employees entails multiple support systems.

The Optimal Ethics Systems Model in Exhibit 2.2 provides a more detailed guide for developing ethical employees, and achieving superior financial performance based on best practices that appear in the business ethics literature.

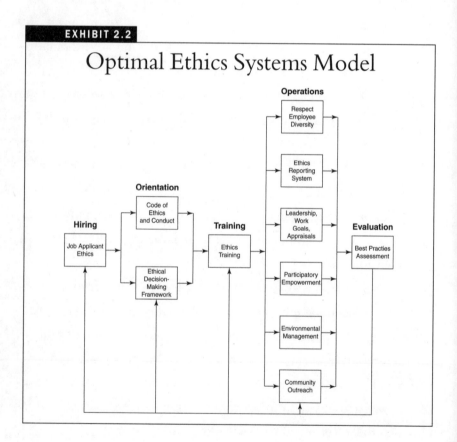

EXHIBIT 2.2

Optimal Ethics Systems Model

Managers should hire ethical job candidates and reinforce ethical behavior throughout the organization. Best practices for each dimension of the model are explained in Chapters 3 through 12. The process consists of:

- Hiring Ethical People (Chapter 3)
- Codes of Ethics and Codes of Conduct (Chapter 4)
- Ethical Decision-Making Framework (Chapter 5)
- Ethics Training (Chapter 6)
- Respecting Employee Diversity (Chapter 7)
- Ethics Reporting Systems (Chapter 8)
- Ethical Leadership, Work Goals, and Performance Appraisals (Chapter 9)
- Empowering Ethical Employees (Chapter 10)
- Environmental Management (Chapter 11)
- Community Outreach and Respect (Chapter 12)

Implementing the Optimal Ethics Systems Model can significantly reduce unethical or illegal behaviors. Human beings, however, will remain morally imperfect and ethical problems can still arise. Depending on the egregiousness of the unethical behavior, the employee should be either disciplined or fired.

These short-term solutions, however, do not address the systematic root of the ethical problem. Why wasn't the employee's unethical proclivity detected earlier? Is there a problem with the hiring process, ethics training workshops, or performance evaluations? Similar to Total Quality Management, the ultimate goal of the Optimal Ethics Systems Model is as close to zero defects as possible.

TIPS AND TECHNIQUES

The Total Quality Management of Ethics

The Total Quality Management of Ethics process provides a systematic approach for determining the root cause of an unethical behavior.

1 Focus on the particular unethical activity the employee did.

2 Instead of merely blaming the particular employee, determine the systematic source that allowed the problem to occur. Did the problem originate from a(n):

a. *Hiring Process Problem*: Was an unethical person hired?

b. *Code of Ethics or Conduct Problem*: Do these codes inadequately address the issue?

c. *Ethical Decision-Making Framework Problem*: Did the employee inadequately apply ethical reasoning to the situation?

d. *Ethics Training Problem*: Does the training program inadequately address the issue?

e. *Ethics Reporting System Problem*: Are the mechanisms for raising ethical issues and reporting unethical behaviors inadequate?

f. *Manager Role Model Problem*: Is the employee's manager an inadequate role model?

g. *Unrealistic Work Goal Problem*: Were the employee's work goals unattainable or misdirected?

h. *Performance Evaluation Problem*: Are performance evaluation measures inadequate?

i. *External Stakeholder Oversight Problem*: Did the regulator or professional association inadequately address the issue?

3 Seek input from affected constituents on how to strategically address the problem.

④ Develop an action plan that includes:

    a. Clearly stated problem

    b. Initial solution to the problem

    c. Major obstacles against implementing the solution

    d. Recommendations for overcoming the obstacles

    e. Development and monitoring metrics to measure success

⑤ Make managers accountable for the results. Senior leaders should set unambiguous objectives and provide the necessary resources and appropriate incentives.

Summary

Unethical business activities are not new. Business owners and managers have always had the freedom to choose to behave ethically or unethically.

In the 1700s, Adam Smith outlined the ethical foundation of capitalism. He maintained that providing individuals with freedom and liberty to pursue their self-interests in the economic sector enhances the wealth of a nation. More people have jobs and a better quality of life. Minimal government intervention would be required, because people are concerned about the well-being of others and they possess a conscience. These psychological mechanisms restrain people from exercising their liberty in a manner that harms others. If these restraints fail, then a system of justice must develop, and enforce, laws that punish those whose unethical behaviors harm others.

The vitality of free-market capitalism depends on ethics. The more ethical people in business behave, the more freedom and liberty government can allow in the economic system. Unethical behavior that reaches a critical level results in new government regulations and oversight mechanisms.

The remainder of this book describes how managers can implement the Optimal Ethics Systems Model to maximize the likelihood of ethical behaviors and minimize the likelihood of unethical behaviors.

Note

1. www.ussc.gov/2005guid/tabconchapt8.htm, accessed 9/16/08.

PART 2

Getting Everyone on Board

CHAPTER 3

Hiring Ethical People

After reading this chapter, you will be able to:

- Screen job candidates for their ethics
- Understand what job candidate factors are illegal to consider when hiring
- Obtain accurate behavior information from resumes, reference checks, background checks, and integrity tests
- Use personality tests scales that measure ethics
- Ask interview questions that address ethical issues
- Conduct alcohol, drug, and polygraph tests

Sometimes, after dismissing an employee for an ethical breach, a manager might wonder: How did that person get through the hiring process?

Hiring just one employee with an unethical value system—someone whose sense of morality and fairness does not match that of a high-integrity work culture—can corrupt an organization. If left alone, the inappropriate hire is likely to attract like-minded people and lead them in directions detrimental to organizational operations.

Efforts to maximize ethical behavior and minimize unethical behavior at work must begin during the hiring process. Hiring someone is inviting the person to join your family, if your organization is small, or your community, if the organization is a larger one. Some people are kind, helpful, trustworthy, and enjoyable, while others are mean-spirited, irritating, dishonest, and annoying.

Many organizations focus on screening for technical skills, not ethical skills. Instead, organizations should implement a hiring process that results in employees who meet four criteria: experience, intellect, energy, and ethics. This chapter provides a five-step process for determining the ethics of job candidates.

The Five-Step Ethics Job Screen Process

A wide range of methods are available to help organizations determine a job candidate's ethics. The five-step Ethics Job Screen Process outlined in Exhibit 3.1 integrates the best practices into a systematic, chronologic framework that complements an organization's job-recruiting process. The first step is a cautionary one, ensuring that any method used to determine ethics does not violate federal law. The next four steps are information sources.

Step 1: Legal Ground Rules

Gather and use information in a way that does not discriminate against job candidates based on their race, color, religion, gender, national origin, age, or disability.

EXHIBIT 3.1

Five-Step Ethics Job Screen

Step	Explanation
1. Legal Ground Rules	Gather and use information in a way that does not discriminate against job candidates based on their race, color, religion, gender, national origin, age, or disability.
2. Behavioral Information	Review behavioral information from resumes, reference checks, background checks, and integrity tests.
3. Personality Traits	Obtain measures for personality traits . . . such as conscientiousness, organizational citizenship behavior, social dominance, and bullying.
4. Interview Questions	Interview the job finalists about their responses to ethical dilemmas experienced at previous workplaces and how they would respond to ethical dilemmas experienced by current employees. In addition, clarify inconsistencies and ambiguities that arise during the previous two job screening steps.
5. Other Tests	Where appropriate, conduct alcohol, drug, and polygraph tests as a final test of the job finalist's integrity.

Good ethics begins with the employer. Employers exemplify good ethics by respecting the law when recruiting and selecting employees. Many federal and state laws govern the types of information an employer can gather on job candidates and the reasons an employer can invoke for selecting one job candidate over another.

Title VII of the Civil Rights Act of 1964 prohibits all businesses from discriminating based on an individual's race, color, religion, gender, or national origin.[1] These groups of previously discriminated people are referred to as "protected classes." Title VII has been expanded to prohibit employers from discriminating based on age and physical or mental disabilities.

The law does not apply to religious organizations or organizations with less than 15 employees. The small business exception applies to a variety of federal regulatory laws so as not to overwhelm these businesses with compliance burdens.

There are two other major exemptions to Title VII:

- If a direct relationship exists between a protected class and an inability to perform the job task
- If the discrimination relates to the "essence" or "central mission" of the employer's business, if it is a bona fide occupational qualification (i.e., a Chinese person applying for a job as a waiter in a Chinese restaurant)

Unlawful discrimination can be apparent on the *front end* of the hiring process, wherein members of protected classes are intentionally excluded from the job candidate pool. Word-of-mouth recruiting, such as recommendations from other employees or colleagues, is often a very effective means of attracting high quality employees. But if the organization has a homogenous workforce consisting of white males, this could result in a job application pool of only white males.

Unlawful discrimination also can be apparent at the *end* of the hiring process. As a rule of thumb, the organization's diversity composition should reflect the demographics of people within a geographic region possessing the necessary job skills and knowledge. Disparate impacts occur when members of a protected class rarely make it through all the job screening filters, suggesting that one of the decision rules could be discriminatory.[2]

Exhibit 3.2 provides a checklist for determining the viability of a job selection rule. A "Yes" response to any of the three rules could result in a discrimination lawsuit. Integrity and personality test vendors should be required to affirm in writing that, based on use by other clients, the instrument has been proven not to violate any of the three rules.

The legal system is equally demanding about the obligations job candidates owe the employer. Job candidates are legally required to respond truthfully to job-related questions on application forms. Insert a sentence directly above the job candidate's signature line stating that:[3]

EXHIBIT 3.2

Job Selection Rule Checklist

Rule	Explanation
1.	Does the selection rule discriminate against job candidates based on their race, color, religion, gender, national origin, or age?
2.	Does the selection rule discriminate against job candidates with physical or mental disabilities?
3.	Does the selection rule result in outcomes in which members of protected classes who live in the geographic region and possess the basic level of education and experience required are disproportionately underrepresented?

1. All answers provided by the job candidate are truthful.

2. Any false or purposely omitted information will lead to the job candidate's disqualification.

3. Any false or purposely omitted information that becomes known after employment will lead to job termination.

Step 2: Behavioral Information

Behavioral information about a job candidate's ethics is more reliable than attitudinal survey results or responses to hypothetical dilemmas.

Four recruiting tools can provide useful behavioral information about a job candidate's ethics: resumes, reference checks, background checks, and integrity tests. Each of them has strengths and weaknesses.

Resumes

The best predictor of future performance is past performance. A job candidate's previous accomplishments are encapsulated on a resume or job application. Typically, resumes contain valuable information about previous work experience and educational attainment, as well as awards received for outstanding performance and community service activities.

Some job candidates stretch the truth, or lie outright, to look good on paper. False information or inconsistencies on resumes are indicative of a person's lack of ethics and trustworthiness.

Researchers estimate that 20–44% of all resumes—more than one in five—contain lies. ADP Screening and Selection Services found that 44% of the resumes they reviewed had lies about work histories, 41% had lies about educational background, and 23% noted fabricated licenses or other credentials.[4]

Even those applying for the highest-level job openings provide misinformation. Jude W. Werra, owner of a headhunting company, publishes an Executive Liar's Index twice a year. Werra reviews the resumes his firm receives for CEO and Vice President job openings and calculates the percentage that contain false educational information. The Executive Liar's Index usually ranges between 10 and 20%.[5]

If false information is detected, notify the job candidate and ask for an explanation of the discrepancy. Correct and forgive innocent mistakes or misunderstandings. More serious infractions serve as a warning about the candidate's willingness to circumvent the truth to gain a competitive advantage. Choose an equally qualified job candidate instead. If none are available, then carefully monitor the new hire until trust has been earned.

Reference Checks

Reference and background checks play an important role in helping prospective employers learn more about the ethics of job candidates.

Job candidates usually list references predisposed to sharing positive information. The most important information an employer can receive is the previous supervisor's perspective of the job candidate's strengths and weaknesses. If it is not listed among the references, request the previous supervisor's contact information and ask the job candidate why the person was not listed. Maybe the supervisor was unethical or might be upset that the employee quit.

For management positions, request the names of previous subordinates as references. An excellent manager would welcome the opportunity to do so. Ask the previous subordinate whether he or she would want to work for this manager again. If it is not possible to contact the subordinate, ask the candidate how a previous subordinate would classify the applicant's strengths and weaknesses.

Some references are hesitant to provide information critical of the job applicant for fear of being sued. Some former employers refuse all reference inquiries, while others will only verify the dates of employment.

Even in this worst case situation, the former supervisor or employer can be asked: "Would you hire this person again?"

References are usually willing to share positive information about a former employee, even if their organization has a strict policy not to divulge anything beyond the basic employment facts. If the contact person responds very favorably to the question, that might be all the information needed. If the contact person hesitates, or refuses to answer, then that too can be valuable information.

References are legally protected from a defamation lawsuit as long as the information being conveyed is truthful. A signed release statement by the job candidate provides the reference with even greater confidence of legal protection against a defamation lawsuit.

TIPS AND TECHNIQUES

Legal Protections for Contacting References[6]

Include a statement on the job application form for the candidate to sign that:

1 Authorizes you to investigate the truthfulness of the information provided

2 Authorizes references, former employers, and educators to respond truthfully about the person's qualifications and character

3 Promises not to hold any of the references liable for conveying truthful information

Background Checks

Conduct background checks to verify a job candidate's educational accomplishments and prior work responsibilities, the two resume areas most prone to lies and exaggerations.

Extensive background checks are legally required for certain high-security jobs, such as those in the financial securities, law enforcement, or healthcare industries. Background checks are also highly recommended when the job entails interacting with the public. Managers can conduct their own informal background checks through Google or contract out for a more formal analysis.

Educational accomplishments are a common resume problem. A background check could reveal that a workshop attended at a local college or university has been inflated to the status of coursework taken toward an advanced degree. A background check can also reveal whether the listed higher education institution is legitimate or an unaccredited diploma mill that provides credentials to people without taking courses.

Other types of background checks include credit checks, criminal records, motor vehicle reports, Social Security verification, and Internet searches.

Credit checks can provide important information about the job candidate's sense of responsibility. Creditworthiness must be job related if the credit check is a determining factor for denying employment. A history of bouncing checks may be relevant for a candidate applying for CFO, but probably not for janitor. Notify the job candidate that a credit check will be conducted, and provide an opportunity to explain any information that raises questions about the individual's credibility.

A list of free public records obtainable over the Internet is available at www.freeprf.com.[7] The FBI, for a modest fee, offers to conduct background checks at www.doj.mt.gov/enforcement/criminaljustice/ backgroundchecks.asp.[8]

A previous arrest record can provide useful information about a job candidate. But in terms of it being a determining factor, the arrest must be job related (e.g., a pharmacist applicant with a drug conviction). A job candidate cited for smoking marijuana during college, however, could be an excellent employee in most other occupations. The arrest should be discussed during the job interview.

The Internet provides additional tools for understanding the ethics of job candidates. MySpace (www.myspace.com) and Facebook (www.facebook.com) are popular social networking Web sites where individuals submit personal information, photos, and videos about themselves. Some Web sites are available for anyone to view, while others require entry approval. These profiles can reveal a great deal about a person's behaviors and attitudes. Some profiles may highlight involvement in community service, while others may contain embarrassing pictures and highly opinionated statements about alcohol or drug consumption.

MySpace and Facebook, initially developed for teenagers and young adults, span all generations. During June 2007, half of

MySpace's 68 million users were 35 years and older, as were 40 percent of Facebook's 26 million users.[9]

Simply "Googling" a job candidate's name can result in a list of Web sites highlighting ethical, or unethical, activities. Be careful when reviewing this information. The Internet is easy to abuse and may contain false information about an individual.

Job candidates should be provided an opportunity to respond to any questionable background check information during the interview process.

Integrity Tests

Integrity tests, also referred to as honesty tests, typically gather information about the job candidate's behaviors and attitudes toward unethical workplace activities, such as theft. Three popular integrity tests are portions of the Reid Report, the Stanton Survey, and the Personnel Selection Inventory (PSI).

Integrity tests may take any of the following four approaches:[10]

1. Direct admission of performing an illegal or questionable activity: "I stole money from my previous employer."

2. Opinions regarding illegal or questionable behavior: "It is okay for people to steal from employers."

3. Personality traits related to dishonesty: "I constantly think about stealing from my employer."

4. Reaction to a hypothetical situation featuring dishonest behavior: "If I saw an employee steal money, I would ignore the situation and wait for the boss to find out."

Researchers have found that individuals with low integrity test scores at the time of employment, compared to those with higher scores, are more likely to later engage in theft, have high absenteeism, break rules, cheat, and become disciplinary problems.[11] In one study, a group of stores using integrity tests experienced a 35% *decline* in inventory loss and 13% *decline* in employee turnover over the next year, while stores not using integrity tests experienced a 10% *increase* in theft and a 14% *increase* in turnover.[12]

Despite these impressive findings, using self-report integrity tests as the sole criteria for hiring people may deny organizations the services of some very honest individuals. Tutorials and coaches are available to help individuals score high on integrity tests. The "best" integrity test answer is often obvious and, as a result, dishonest individuals who lie can score higher than honest individuals.

For example, a common integrity test statement is: "I am a trustworthy person." A dishonest person wanting the job would lie by choosing "Strongly Agree." An individual of high integrity, fully aware of personal imperfections, might choose "Agree" rather than "Strongly Agree," resulting in a lower score.

Integrity tests signal to job candidates that ethics matter and dishonest individuals may decide to withdraw their application. Due to social desirability concerns—the likelihood of liars scoring higher than honest people—corroborate integrity test scores with other ethics measures and discuss the results during the job interview.

Step 3: Personality Traits

Obtain measures for personality traits such as conscientiousness, organizational citizenship behavior, and social dominance and bullying.

Conscientiousness

Of the hundreds of possible personality measures, "conscientiousness" is the best predictor of ethics and job performance. Individuals who behave ethically also tend to be responsible, dependable, and hardworking. This is particularly noteworthy because conscientiousness is a strong predictor of job performance.[13]

As with integrity tests, personality tests can be prone to eliciting socially desirable answers because the desired character trait being measured is somewhat obvious. Conscientiousness scores can be verified with a reference check.

Organizational Citizenship Behavior

Organizational citizenship behavior (OCB) refers to helping behaviors that go beyond normal job requirements, such as aiding others with their job-related problems. OCB is most often measured using five factors: altruism, courtesy, civic virtue, conscientiousness, and sportsmanship.

Researchers report that individuals who score high on OCB also score high for task effectiveness, and being optimistic and team-oriented.[14]

Social Dominance and Bullying

Ethics demands sincere, open-minded, respectful conversations with a wide variety of people about alternative actions under consideration. Social dominance orientation (SDO) is the belief that an individual's particular group membership (defined in terms of race, gender, religion, or ethnicity) is superior to other groups. Researchers have found high SDO scores associated with racism and sexism. SDO survey items include: "To get ahead in life, it is sometimes necessary to step on other groups" and "Inferior groups should stay in their place."[15]

A survey of U.S. workers found that approximately 30% were bullied by a boss or co-worker.[16] The two most common forms of bullying were having information held that affected job performance and being exposed to an unmanageable workload. Researchers report that a predisposition to bullying others is also associated with racial and gender discrimination.

In the Real World: Mark-to-Market Accounting—1991 provides a modern example of this phenomenon. Enron's Jeff Skilling had a reputation for bullying subordinates, external auditors, and government regulators. He knew what he wanted and would not take "no" for an answer. His strong will led to both his success and his downfall.

IN THE REAL WORLD

Mark-to-Market Accounting—1991

Ken Lay approved Jeff Skilling's innovative proposal, created a Gas Bank Division, and hired Skilling to be the new division's CEO. The Gas Bank was immediately successful. By the end of 1990, Enron's annual revenue rocketed up to $13.2 billion, a 40% increase from the previous year. But the value of Enron's stock did not reflect this change.

The Gas Bank division operated more like a financial institution than a traditional gas pipeline company. Skilling maintained that stock market investors failed to realize the Gas Bank's true economic value because the division had to use the traditional oil-and-gas accounting system. Instead, he wanted to use the financial industry's mark-to-market accounting system. Mark-to-market would allow the Gas Bank to immediately claim anticipated long-term revenue when a contract was signed, rather than waiting until the revenue was actually received during the length of the contract. The financial difference would be huge.

Changing the accounting system required approval from the Securities and Exchange Commission (SEC). The SEC rejected Enron's initial proposal because of the potential for pricing manipulations. Skilling countered that diligent auditor oversight would prevent price manipulations. Enron's auditor was Arthur Andersen, one of the most prestigious accounting firms in the world. Arthur Andersen agreed to write a letter to the SEC supporting the Gas Bank's use of a mark-to-market accounting system. The final decision to appeal the SEC ruling was up to Ken Lay.

DECISION CHOICE. If you were the CEO of Enron, would you:

❶ Keep the traditional oil-and-gas accounting system for Skilling's Gas Bank division?

❷ Appeal the SEC rejection and resubmit a proposal for adopting a mark-to-market accounting system for the Gas Bank division?

Why?

Step 4: Interview Questions

Interview job finalists about their responses to ethical dilemmas experienced at previous workplaces, and how they would respond to ethical dilemmas experienced by current employees. In addition, clarify inconsistencies and ambiguities that arose during the previous job screening steps.

The ethics questions about previous work experiences must be job-related, and a standardized format followed, to avoid protected-class biases. Questions that can be asked include:

- Have you ever observed an employee or customer stealing product? How did you respond?

- Have you ever observed an employee sexually harassing another employee or customer? How did you respond?

- Have you ever observed anything at work, or done anything at work, that violated industry standards or the law? How did you respond?

- Have you ever been asked by a boss, coworker, customer, or supplier to do something unethical? How did you respond?

- Have you ever observed anything at work, or done anything at work, that bothered your conscience? How did you respond?

Asking job candidates to describe how they managed an ethical dilemma at a previous employer can provide very useful information. Human beings are creatures of habit, and the job candidate will be bringing his or her ethical dilemma response patterns to the new place of employment.

If the person claims not to have previously experienced any ethical dilemmas, then transform the issue into a hypothetical situation: "How would you respond if you observed someone stealing?"

Sensitize job candidates to real-life ethical dilemmas current employees have experienced and ask how they would respond. The job interviewer can develop these dilemmas based on his or her own experience, or have current employees compose them as an ethics training workshop activity (see Chapter 6). Current employees should develop three distinct responses to each ethical dilemma scenario they compose, and then rank them according to the most ethical response, a moderate ethical response, and the least ethical response.

These types of interview questions or scenarios may generate dishonest responses from the job candidate if the most ethical answer is obvious: "Of course I would report a boss or coworker embezzling money!"

Unfortunately, there is no one clear behavioral indicator that differentiates liars from honest people. Interviewers typically overestimate their ability to detect lies. Even the best-trained professionals are only accurate 64–73% of the time. What an interviewer might assume to be a verbal or bodily cue for lying—a long pause before answering, avoiding eye contact, shaking of a foot, or rubbing of hands—may instead be a sign of shyness or nervousness. Pointing out this behavioral response to an ethics question can provide useful information.

Step 5: Other Tests—Alcohol, Drug, and Polygraph Tests

Where appropriate, conduct alcohol, drug, and polygraph tests as a final test of the job finalist's integrity.

Individuals who abuse alcohol and drugs are likely to bring these problems with them to the workplace and are in need of treatment and recovery. Some research studies have found that alcohol and drug use negatively impacts productivity, workplace safety, and employee morale, and can damage a company's reputation in the community. Alcohol and drug tests are easy to conduct and relatively inexpensive.

Alcohol Testing

The National Council on Alcoholism and Drug Dependence reports that 6.6% of full-time employees are heavy drinkers.[17] The highest percentage of heavy drinkers consists of unemployed adults ages 26–34, who are likely looking for employment. Alcoholics and problem drinkers are absent from work four to eight times more often than other employees. Alcoholism can also cause psychological problems, such as aggressiveness, violence, depression, memory loss, and irrationality.

The job interviewer's challenge is determining whether a candidate is an alcoholic or just a moderate drinker. Excessive alcohol consumption over an extended period of time can be determined by urine and blood tests.

A new type of test measures chronic alcoholism by using biological indicators called "biomarkers" that remain elevated for several days after drinking has stopped.[18] These tests are considered 20 times better at detecting heavy drinking than urine analysis.

A breathalyzer test measures the concentration of alcohol in an individual's blood system. But this method does not detect an alcoholic who happens to be sober at the time of the job interview.

The World Health Organization has developed the Alcohol Use Disorders Identification Test (AUDIT) questionnaire to help determine whether a person is an alcoholic.[19] However, self-report surveys are prone to false information because denial is a common response to inquiries about alcohol addiction. For example, problem drinkers seeking employment are unlikely to admit that they need a drink first thing in the morning, which is an AUDIT survey question.

Drug Testing

According to the U.S. Department of Health and Human Services, 9.4 million working Americans use illicit drugs. The typical illegal drug user is a low-paid white male between the ages of 18 and 25.[20] Industries with the highest rates of illicit drug use are food preparation, restaurants and bars, construction, and transportation.

Research studies have found that substance abuse lowers productivity, causes accidents and injuries at work, and increases absenteeism, turnover, workers' compensation claims, and medical costs. Drugs impair an individual's judgment, which puts the life of other employees or customers at risk. Drug abusers are also more likely to steal from employers to pay for their expensive drug habits. Some companies in the transportation industry, and those with large federal contracts, are required by law to conduct drug tests.

Drug use can be determined by an analysis of blood, urine, hair, or saliva. Marijuana, the most commonly tested-for drug, can be detected in the blood system for two days, in urine from 2–14 days, and in hair follicles for up to 90 days. Each method has its own set of strengths and weaknesses.

Urinalysis is the most often used method for pre-employment drug testing. It is also the most personally invasive. A closely observed urine collection process can be a degrading experience. But if not closely observed, job candidates can switch samples or change the composition of the urine through detox products.

Hair testing is less invasive than urinalysis and has greater validity. A strand of hair contains an individual's drug history during the lifetime of that hair. However, it takes longer to obtain laboratory results from hair tests.

Analyzing saliva is noninvasive, easy to collect, and results can be obtained in a few minutes. But saliva is useful only for determining drug use during the previous two days, after which drug traces are no longer contained in saliva.

Polygraphs

Polygraphs, also known as lie detectors, can be used as a job screen by federal, state, and local government agencies, as well as businesses, engaged in national security issues.[21]

The modern polygraph collects data on at least three physiological systems associated with honesty and lying: respiration, sweat gland activity, and blood pressure. Polygraphs can be very valid with a skilled operator, with accuracy rates ranging from 81 to 98%. But the results do not provide absolute proof because polygraphs directly detect nervousness and only indirectly detect lying. Many Web sites suggest ways to beat the polygraph, but polygraph experts maintain that these methods can be detected by a skilled polygraph administrator.

Inaccuracies, and abuse of polygraph testing by employers, resulted in the Employee Polygraph Protection Act of 1988. The law prohibits pre-employment polygraph tests for most other public and private companies except pharmaceutical and security companies.

Even if a polygraph is 99% accurate, 1 out of 100 individuals may inappropriately be denied employment if the test results are the sole determining factor. Legal action can be taken by an innocent person denied employment due to inaccurate lie detection results.

Given their high validity rates, employers should use polygraphs when permitted by law, such as situations involving national security issues. Reference checks and other methods for appraising the ethics of job candidates take on greater significance if a job candidate strongly contests the polygraph findings.

Summary

Organizations should apply a five-step ethics job screen to determine the ethics of job candidates. The best measures of ethics include:

- Behavior information from resumes, reference checks, background checks, and integrity tests
- Survey instrument scales measuring personality traits such as conscientiousness, organizational citizenship behavior, social dominance orientation, and bullying
- Interview questions that explore previous ethical dilemmas at work
- Alcohol, drug, and polygraph tests

Applying the five-step ethics job screen process demonstrates a significant effort by a company to evaluate the ethics of job candidates and sends a strong message to both job candidates and current employees that ethics matter.

Notes

1. Bernard Grofman (ed.), *Legacies of the 1964 Civil Rights Act* (Charlottesville, VA: University of Virginia Press, 2000).

2. A free disparate impact analysis calculator is available online at www.hr-software.net/EmploymentStatistics/DisparateImpact. htm, accessed 9/4/08.

3. Bradden C. Backer, Kim E. Patterson, and Robert K. Scholl, *Hiring and Firing in Wisconsin* (Madison, WI: State Bar of Wisconsin CLE Books, 1996), Section 2.20.

4. Susan Bowles, "Background Checks: Beware and Be Prepared," *USA Today*, April 10, 2002.

5. Joe Dresang, "Just the Facts," *Milwaukee Journal Sentinel*, April 5, 2007.

6. Bradden C. Backer, Kim E. Patterson, and Robert K. Scholl, *Hiring and Firing in Wisconsin* (Madison, WI: State Bar of Wisconsin CLE Books, 1996), Section 2.22.

7. Accessed 9/4/08.

8. Accessed 9/4/08.

9. Maha Atal, "MySpace, Facebook: A Tale of Two Cultures," *Business Week Online*, July 2, 2007.

10. Kevin R. Murphy, *Honesty in the Workplace* (Pacific Grove, CA: Brooks/Cole, 1993).

11. Christopher M. Berry, Paul R. Sackett, and Shelly Wiemann, "A Review of Recent Developments in Integrity Test Research," *Personnel Psychology*, 36, no. 5 (2007): 1097–1108.

12. James Krohe, Jr., "Are Workplace Tests Worth Taking?" *Across the Board*, 43, no. 4 (2006): 16–23.

13. http://ipip.ori.org/newBigFive5broadKey.htm#Conscientious ness, accessed 9/5/08.

14. Mark C. Bolina and William H. Trunley, "Going the Extra Mile: Cultivating and Managing Employee Citizenship Behavior," *Academy of Management Executive*, 2003, 17, no. 3: 60–71.

15. Jim Sidanius and Felicia Pratto, *Social Dominance: An Intergroup Theory of Social Hierarchy and Oppression* (New York: Cambridge University Press, 2001).

16. Pamela Lutgen-Sandvik, Sarah J. Tracy, and Jess K. Alberts, "Burned by Bullying in the American Workplace: Prevalence, Perception, Degree and Impact," *Journal of Management Studies*, 44, no. 6 (2007): 837–862.

17. www.ncadd.org/facts/workplac.html, accessed 9/5/08; a heavy drinker is defined as drinking five or more drinks per occasion on five or more days in the past 30 days.

18. Pamela Bean, "State of the Art: Contemporary Biomarkers of Alcohol Consumption," *Medical Laboratory Observer*, November 2005.

19. Thomas F. Babor, John C. Higgins-Biddle, John B. Saunders, and Maristela G. Monteiro, *AUDIT: The Alcohol Use Disorders Identification Test* (Geneva, Switzerland: World Health Organization).

20. http://workplace.samhsa.gov/DrugTesting/Files_Drug_Testing/ FactSheet/factsheet041906.aspx, accessed 9/5/08.

21. Committee to Review the Scientific Evidence on the Polygraph, *The Polygraph and Lie Detection* (Washington, D.C.: The National Academies Press, 2003).

CHAPTER 4

Codes of Ethics and Codes of Conduct

After reading this chapter, you will be able to:

- Explain the importance of code awareness and expectations
- Describe the content found in most Codes of Ethics and Codes of Conduct
- Develop an effective code
- Conduct an annual employee assessment of the Code of Ethics
- Use the assessment survey feedback to develop continuous improvement changes

The perfect job candidate has been hired—the person is experienced, energetic, intelligent, and has high integrity. However, people of high integrity do not necessarily share the same ethical viewpoints. What bothers one person's conscience may not bother another person's conscience.

Each person develops a unique ethical viewpoint, a perspective shaped by parents, siblings, friends, teachers, religious leaders, political leaders, other moral role models, and culture. Ethical dilemmas arise because situations are ambiguous, and two people of high integrity might disagree on the best ethical response.

An organization's Code of Ethics and Code of Conduct minimize ethical ambiguities by communicating guidelines for employees to apply when making decisions. They serve as the organization's conscience. This chapter explains the differences between a Code of Ethics and a Code of Conduct, summarizes their prevalence and content, and describes how to use a Code of Ethics to assess and improve ethical performance.

Difference Between a Code of Ethics and a Code of Conduct

A Code of Ethics and a Code of Conduct are two unique documents. A Code of Ethics describes broad ethical aspirations. A Code of Conduct describes acceptable behaviors for specific situations that are likely to arise.

A Code of Ethics is like the Ten Commandments, a few general principles to guide behavior that could fit on one piece of paper or a business card. The general principles embodied in a Code of Ethics—such as respecting all owners, customers, employees, suppliers, community members, and the natural environment—represent aspirations. These principles describe the kind of people we want to be, such as a person who respects everybody.

A Code of Conduct provides substance to the Code of Ethics and is usually several pages long. A Code of Conduct applies the Code of Ethics to a host of relevant situations. Whereas one principle in the Code of Ethics might state that all employees will obey the law, a Code of Conduct might list several specific laws relevant to organizational operations that employees will obey.

For instance, the Code of Ethics of the National Association of Social Workers (NASW) lists six ethical principles to guide behavior: service, social justice, dignity and worth of the person, importance of human relationships, integrity, and competence.[1] The more detailed NASW Code of Conduct explains that social workers will obtain informed consent from clients regarding the purpose of services provided, relevant costs, and treatment alternatives. The NASW Code of Conduct also addresses situations involving conflicts of interest, confidentiality, access to records, sexual relationships, sexual harassment, derogatory language, and termination of services.

Importance of Code Expectations and Awareness

Codes of Ethics and Conduct demonstrate managerial concern about ethics, convey a particular set of values to all employees, and have an impact on employee behavior. They provide employees with clear and consistent moral guidance.

Despite all these benefits, researchers report that many companies have a vague Code of Ethics that is not well-communicated to employees.[2] The organization's leadership team must communicate the importance of these codes to employees and make them readily available.

From a very practical perspective, codes are essential, because a manager may be unavailable to discuss an ethical issue that arises among subordinates, unreceptive to discussing ethical issues, or a bad role model. Employees need a reliable source of information to guide them when ethical issues arise.

Prevalence of Codes of Ethics and Conduct

Many organizations have a Code of Ethics. Public companies are required to do so by law. Private companies do so because it is a best practice and in response to market or stakeholder expectations. Codes of Ethics are also prevalent in the government sector.

Following an onslaught of high-profile corporate scandals involving Enron, WorldCom, and Arthur Andersen, Congress quickly passed the Sarbanes-Oxley Act of 2002. The legislation required all publicly traded companies to disclose whether they had a Code of Ethics for senior financial officers. The New York Stock Exchange (NYSE) and the National Association of Securities Dealers Automated Quotations (NASDAQ) went one step further. To gain renewed investor confidence in the stock market, they required that all listed firms must have a Code of Ethics for directors, officers, and employees.[3]

Codes of Ethics and Conduct for particular professions establish legal obligations to behave ethically. These professional codes safeguard members against managerial pressure to behave unethically and are applicable to all organizations. Lawyers, accountants, teachers, and social workers who violate their professional code could lose their license.

There are also Codes of Ethics for conducting business internationally. The Caux Round Table, an international network of business leaders wanting to promote moral capitalism, published a list of seven principles, based on the concepts of common good and human dignity, to guide international corporate behavior.[4]

Code of Ethics Content

A Code of Ethics, sometimes referred to as a Values Statement, expresses the principles that define an organization's ideal moral essence. Keep the language simple and avoid legalese or professional jargon. The code should be easy to understand and inspirational, something that unites employees regardless of their particular religion, ethnicity, gender, or geographical location.

The tone of an ethics code is very important. Providing employees with a list of things they should not do feels oppressive rather than inspirational. A Code of Ethics should be affirmative, stating how people *should* act. Declaring that employees will always tell the truth, rather than will not lie, creates positive expectations.

An extensive review of corporate Codes of Ethics, global Codes of Ethics, and the business ethics literature found the following six universal moral values continually expressed:[5]

1. *Trustworthiness*

2. *Respect*

3. *Responsibility*

4. *Fairness*

5. *Caring*

6. *Citizenship*

Exhibit 4.1 provides an example of a Code of Ethics that highlights four guiding principles: open communication, respect for others, personal integrity, and performance excellence.

Have employees participate in constructing the code. Examples from other companies can serve as a starting point. A cross-functional team, representing different aspects of company operations, can then draft a code for managerial approval. The end result is a unique Code of Ethics with a broad base of support.

EXHIBIT 4.1

Code of Ethics

OUR VALUES

Communication

We have an obligation to communicate. Here, we take the time to talk with one another . . . and to listen. We believe that information is meant to move and that information moves people.

Respect

We treat others as we would like to be treated ourselves. We do not tolerate abusive or disrespectful treatment. Ruthlessness, callousness, and arrogance don't belong here.

Integrity

We work with customers and prospects openly, honestly, and sincerely. When we say we will do something, we will do it; when we say we cannot or will not do something, then we won't do it.

Excellence

We are satisfied with nothing less than the very best in everything we do. We will continue to raise the bar for everyone. The
great fun here will be for all of us to discover just how good we
can really be.

Code of Conduct Content

A Code of Conduct expands on the moral principles embodied in a
Code of Ethics. A Code of Ethics principle such as "We will treat
everyone fairly," for example, can be clarified in a Code of Conduct
as "All information about an employee is considered confidential and
is to be released only to authorized personnel."

Creating a Code of Conduct requires input from top-level executives, corporate lawyers, and human resource personnel. The code
should address the wide range of legal expectations and ethical risks
unique to the organization or job title. Revise the Code of Conduct
when new issues arise

The NYSE recommends that a Code of Conduct address seven
topics:[6]

1. *Conflicts of Interest.* Avoid conflict or potential conflict between
   an individual's personal interests and those of the organization.

2. *Corporate Opportunities.* Do not use corporate information or
   assets for personal gain.

3. *Confidentiality.* Do not disclose nonpublic information that
   could benefit competitors or harm the organization.

4. *Fair Dealing.* Abstain from any unfair treatment of customers, suppliers, competitors, and employees, such as concealment, abuse of privileged information, and misrepresentation of material facts.

5. *Protection and Proper Use of Assets.* Use assets efficiently and avoid theft, carelessness, and waste.

6. *Compliance with Laws, Rules, and Regulations.* Proactively promote compliance.

7. *Encouraging the Reporting of Any Illegal or Unethical Behavior.* Proactively promote ethical behavior and do not allow retaliation for reports made in good faith.

Develop different Codes of Conduct for different work functions. For instance, scholars conducted an extensive review of human resource management issues and found five ethical issues—misrepresentation and collusion, misuse of data, manipulation and coercion, value and goal conflict, and technical ineptness—that are uniquely experienced in each of the eight HR functions—staffing and selection, employee and career development, labor relations, compensation and benefits, safety and health, organization development, HR planning, and performance management.[7]

TIPS AND TECHNIQUES

A Code of Conduct for Suppliers

Some organizations create codes of conduct for external stakeholders. Starbucks' suppliers must sign a Code of Conduct pledging that the supplier:[8]

- Demonstrates commitment to the welfare, economic improvement, and sustainability of the people and places that produce Starbucks' products and services

- Adheres to local laws and international standards regarding human rights, workplace safety, and worker compensation and treatment

- Meets or exceeds national laws and international standards for environmental protection

- Commits to measuring, monitoring, reporting, and verifying compliance

- Pursues continuous improvement of these social and environmental principles

Effective Codes

The Code of Ethics in Exhibit 4.1 highlights a problem with codes: Words are meaningless unless they correspond with actions. The code was developed by Enron a decade prior to the company's financial collapse.[9] At Enron, key employees ignored, rather than obeyed, the company's Code of Ethics, particularly when it interfered with new revenue streams (see *In the Real World: The SPE Revenue Solution—1993*).

IN THE REAL WORLD

The SPE Revenue Solution—1993

Ken Lay chose to appeal the SEC's decision to reject the Gas Bank Division's use of mark-to-market accounting techniques. The appeal was successful. Unfortunately, beginning in 1993

(Continued)

this new accounting technique contributed to a cash flow problem for the Gas Bank, because reported revenue was mostly projected, not actual. In addition, Wall Street analysts increased Enron's revenue expectations based on the previous year's reported revenue, which created a need for bigger revenue deals.

Jeff Skilling hired Andy Fastow, a finance expert, to help Enron manage this revenue problem. One of Fastow's revenue ideas was to bundle the Gas Bank's loans and sell them at a discounted price to third parties. This had two benefits: It reduced Enron's debt and increased reported revenue.

Fastow targeted special purpose entities (SPEs) as potential purchasers of the Gas Bank's bundled loans. In the energy industry, SPEs are created to reduce risk associated with natural gas exploration. SPEs have two very important accounting regulations: First, at least 3% of an SPE's funding must come from an external partner, and second, the SPE must be managed by an independent management team.

Fastow planned to finance these SPEs primarily with Enron stock and, when needed, meet Enron's financial targets by selling Gas Bank loans to the SPE. Enron's stock would become more attractive to investors because revenue targets were met and the company's debt-to-equity ratio improved. An increase in Enron's stock price would also directly increase the SPE's economic value, because the SPE owned substantial amounts of Enron stock. Fastow would promise to repurchase the loans from the SPE at a guaranteed profit if the SPE could not resell the loans to other parties. All Fastow needed were some compliant outside SPE investors and managers.

Many investment banks profited from funding Enron's Gas Bank activities and planned on funding Enron's future acquisitions. Fastow ranked investment banks according to Tier 1, Tier 2, and Tier 3 status, with Tier 1 being the banks that received the largest fees from doing business with the Gas Bank. Fastow told Tier

1 investment bankers that they had to invest in and manage his SPEs or they would no longer be considered when the Gas Bank needed more capital.

DECISION CHOICE. If you were a Tier 1 investment banker earning large fees by doing business with Enron's Gas Bank, and Andy Fastow asked you to invest in an SPE that would purchase bundled Gas Banks loans at a guaranteed profit, would you:

❶ Accept the offer?

❷ Reject the offer and lose future fees from Enron?

❸ Notify Arthur Andersen auditors about these secret side agreements?

Why?

Creating Codes of Ethics and Conduct must be followed by effective implementation. Effective implementation of a code increases employee job satisfaction and organizational commitment, enhances ethical performance, and impacts how employees assess the organization's ethics.[10] Hypocrisy sets in if the codes are merely empty words, resulting in a decrease in employee job satisfaction and an increase in employee turnover.

Effective implementation requires support from senior managers, employee training, and management enforcement. Widely distribute the codes and accompany them with a letter signed by a high-level executive that emphasizes the importance of applying the codes on a daily basis. Display the codes in newsletters, Web sites, and highly traveled areas. Employees should sign the codes after they have been introduced during orientation or an ethics training workshop.

Employees are more likely to report a code violation if they do not fear retribution for reporting, others in the organization disapprove of the violation, or the person committing the violation has been given a previous warning.

Social pressure can be a major obstacle to code effectiveness. Employees are very hesitant to report code violations committed by their friends or manager. In addition, unethical employees accuse others of being "tattle-tales" to discourage them from reporting a code violation. Codes must be strongly stated and enforced so that well-meaning employees can overcome these obstacles and either confront coworkers engaged in unethical activities or inform management.

Annual Code of Ethics Assessment

The last phase of implementation is probably the most important— use the code as an organizational assessment tool. Make the Code of Ethics a living document by annually assessing how well the organization and its employees live up to it. Then use the employee feedback as the basis for continuous improvement changes in organizational policies and practices.

Exhibit 4.2 provides a nine-step process for assessing an organization's ethical performance based on its Code of Ethics. The employee activity can be accomplished within 60 to 90 minutes.

It is relatively easy to transform a Code of Ethics into a five-point Likert scale survey for employee assessment purposes. Exhibit 4.3 is a Code of Ethics that describes an organization's five core values.[11]

EXHIBIT 4.2

Code of Ethics Employee Assessment

Step 1 Form small groups around common job tasks and have participants read the organization's Code of Ethics. If none exists, inform participants that organizational members are expected to treat owners, company property, employees, customers, suppliers, the government, and the natural environment with utmost respect and integrity.

Step 2 Each group member independently evaluates how well the organization meets each of the code's ethical aspirations using a five-point Likert scale.

Step 3 Each group member independently highlights one weak area and writes down actions that can be taken to improve that score.

Step 4 Group members share their survey scores with each other and determine similarities and differences.

Step 5 Each group member shares a story about the survey item with the highest score. What happened during the past year that exemplifies why the organization is doing so well in that category?

Step 6 Each group member shares a story about a survey item with a low score and action steps that would improve the low score. Then integrate ideas and suggestions from other group members to develop a more detailed continuous improvement plan.

Step 7 The group summarizes its scores and suggestions for improvement and submits the information to the facilitator for the purpose of continuous improvement follow-up.

Step 8 The facilitator forwards the information to the responsible manager.

Step 9 Management, or the facilitator, updates employees about progress made regarding the suggested improvements.

EXHIBIT 4.3

Code of Ethics

Core Values

Operate with integrity and respect

Integrity means acting in an ethical and honest manner. Respect requires showing patience and acknowledging differences with civility. We expect you to act respectfully and with integrity in all business situations, whether inside or outside the office.

Provide, promote, and celebrate Legendary Service

You are responsible for providing products and services that meet or exceed the expectations of our business partners.

Use superior communications

All of your communications must be professional, courteous, and prompt.

Embrace continuous improvement

Change being constant and necessary, you must embrace opportunities to become more efficient and productive.

Actively engage in self-management

Assume responsibility for self-management at work by assessing your own performance daily, advancing your professional growth, and improving your confidence in your ability to provide Legendary Service.

Exhibit 4.4 transforms the Code of Ethics in Exhibit 4.3 into a survey instrument. The survey differentiates the evaluation of managers from nonmanagement employees because of their different responsibilities and activities.

EXHIBIT 4.4

Code of Ethics Survey

Living Up To The Values Statement

Instructions: Please use the 1–5 scale below to assess how well each of the following statements exemplifies managers and nonmanagement employees. The more honest you are, the more helpful the information we will receive. First assess the behavior of managers, and then the nonmanagement employees.

1=*Strongly Disagree*; 2=*Disagree*; 3=*Neither Agree nor Disagree*; 4=*Agree*; 5=*Strongly Agree*

	SD	D	N	A	SA
Managers					
Operate with integrity and respect	1	2	3	4	5
Provide and promote Legendary Service (meet and exceed customer expectations)	1	2	3	4	5
Use superior communications (are professional, courteous, and prompt)	1	2	3	4	5
Embrace continuous improvement (become more productive and efficient)	1	2	3	4	5
Actively engage in self-management (assess their performance daily)	1	2	3	4	5
Managers Subtotal—Add the five scores and divide by five:					
Nonmanagement Employees					
Operate with integrity and respect	1	2	3	4	5
Provide and promote Legendary Service (meet and exceed customer expectations)	1	2	3	4	5

(Continued)

EXHIBIT 4.4

Nonmanagement Employees (continued)

Use superior communications (are professional, courteous, and prompt)	1	2	3	4	5
Embrace continuous improvement (become more productive and efficient)	1	2	3	4	5
Actively engage in self-management (assess their performance daily)	1	2	3	4	5

Nonmanagement Employees Subtotal — Add the five scores and divide by five:

Assessment of Managers

1. Provide an example of how *managers* live up to the company's Values Statement.

2. Provide an example of how *managers* fall short of living up to the company's Values Statement.

3. How can the company improve the shortcoming noted in #2?

Assessment of Nonmanagement Employees

4. Provide an example of how *nonmanagement employees* live up to the company's Values Statement.

5. Provide an example of how *nonmanagement employees* fall short of living up to the company's Values Statement.

6. How can the company improve the shortcoming noted in #5?

Summary

Employees arrive at the organization with a wide variety of ethical perspectives. They need a common ethical reference point. Develop a Code of Ethics that consists of several general moral principles and a more detailed Code of Conduct that consists of relevant situations that demonstrate these ethical expectations. These codes serve as the organization's conscience.

Make these codes meaningful and effective by using them as assessment tools. Have employees annually assess how well members of the organization live up to these codes. In the spirit of continuous improvement, gather employee suggestions for improving ethical performance and make appropriate changes in organizational policies and practices.

Notes

1. www.socialworkers.org/pubs/code/code.asp, accessed 9/6/08.
2. Denis Collins, "The Quest to Improve the Human Condition: The First 1,500 Articles in the *Journal of Business Ethics*," *Journal of Business Ethics,* 26, no. 1 (2000): 1–73.
3. Randy Myers, "Ensuring Ethical Effectiveness," *Journal of Accountancy,* 195, no. 2 (2003): 28–33.
4. www.cauxroundtable.org/documents/Principles%20for%20Business.PDF, accessed 9/6/08.
5. Mark S. Schwartz, "Universal Moral Values for Corporate Codes of Ethics," *Journal of Business Ethics*, 59, no. 1 (2005): 27–44.
6. Curtis C. Verschoor, "The Ethical Climate Barometer," *Internal Auditor,* 61, no. 5 (2004): 48–53.
7. Kevin C. Wooten, "Ethical Dilemmas in Human Resource Management: An Application of a Multidimensional Framework, a Unifying Taxonomy, and Applicable Codes," *Human Resource Management Review*, 11, no. 1 (2001): 159–176.
8. Sandra Waddock, *Leading Corporate Citizens: Vision, Values, Value Added* (New York: McGraw-Hill Irwin, 2006), 22.

9. *Enron Annual Report 1998* (Houston, TX: Enron, 1998): 71, http://picker.uchicago.edu/Enron/EnronAnnualReport1998.pdf, accessed 8/15/08.

10. Randi L. Sims, "The Relationship Between Employee Attitudes and Conflicting Expectations for Lying Behavior," *The Journal of Psychology,* 134, no. 6 (2000): 619–633.

11. National Specialty Insurance (NSI), a division of West Bend Mutual Insurance Company, "Core Value Statement," www.national-specialty.com/Common/ASPDocuments/default.asp, accessed 9/6/08.

CHAPTER 5

Ethical Decision-Making Framework

After reading this chapter, you will be able to:

- Apply several sets of ethics questions to business issues
- Use a systematic ethics decision-making framework to arrive at moral conclusions
- Understand the five most important ethical theories
- Persuade others by speaking in their ethical language
- Facilitate a negotiation between competing ethical perspectives
- Recognize warning signs that an unethical decision is approaching

Codes of Conduct cannot cover every business situation that might arise. Employees need to know how to independently derive a moral answer to business issues. Several frameworks are available to help employees understand the ethical basis of their decisions and actions.

This chapter summarizes two common ethical decision-making frameworks and then offers a systemic six-question ethics decision-making framework grounded in moral philosophy. A process for persuading people who approach a decision from a different ethical perspective and warning signs that an unethical situation is arising are also provided. The material in this chapter can also be used as the basis of an ethics workshop.

Rotary International's Four-Way Test

How do you know if the decision you are about to make is ethical? A simple framework for analyzing the ethical dimension of a decision is Rotary International's Four-Way Test. More than 1.2 million business, professional, and community leaders are members of Rotary International, and there are more than 32,000 Rotary clubs around the world. In 1943, the Rotary adopted the following Code of Ethics, referred to as The Four-Way Test:[1]

Of the things we think, say, or do:

1. Is it the TRUTH?

2. Is it FAIR to all concerned?

3. Will it build GOODWILL and BETTER FRIENDSHIPS?

4. Will it be BENEFICIAL to all concerned?

Raytheon's Ethics Quick Test

Raytheon provides its employees with an Ethics Quick Test, consisting of the following questions to consider when facing an ethical dilemma:[2]

- Is the action legal?
- Is it right?
- Who will be affected?
- Does it fit Raytheon's values?
- How will I feel afterwards?
- How would it look in the newspaper?
- Will it reflect poorly on the company?

The Ethics Decision-Making Framework

The Rotary's Four-Way Test and Raytheon's Ethics Quick Test are very helpful lists of questions, yet not philosophically systematic.

The moral philosophy literature provides a more systematic approach for deriving moral conclusions. Ethical reasoning is just like any other managerial problem-solving process. When confronting a problem, managers typically list the available options and determine which alternative makes the most sense. The same decision-making process can be applied to ethical reasoning.

Strong consensus, though not absolute agreement, exists among philosophers that some ethical reasons are more morally acceptable than others. For example, it has been long established that "doing to others as you would want done to you" takes precedence over an individual's self-interests when these two ethical theories are in conflict, although some hard-core libertarians might object. This ranking of ethical principles can be found in all cultures.

Exhibit 5.1 provides an ethics decision-making framework that parallels Lawrence Kohlberg's stages of moral reasoning.[3]

An Ethics Decision–Making Framework

Instructions: Answer Questions 1 through 6 to gather the information necessary for performing an ethical analysis. Based on this information, develop a decision that has the strongest ethical basis.

1. Who are all the people affected by the action?

2. Is the action beneficial to me?

3. Is the action supported by my social group?

4. Is the action supported by national laws?

5. Is the action for the greatest good of the greatest number of people affected by it?

6. Are the motives behind the action based on truthfulness and respect/integrity toward each stakeholder?

- *If answers to Questions 2 through 6 are all "yes,"* then do it.

- *If answers to Questions 2 through 6 are all "no,"* then do not do it.

- *If answers to Questions 2 through 6 are mixed,* then modify your decision.

  - *If answers to Questions 5 and 6 are "yes,"* this action is the *most* ethical. You may need to modify this decision in consideration of any "no" answer to Questions 2 through 4.

  - *If answers to Questions 5 and 6 are "no,"* this action is the *least* ethical. Modify this decision in consideration of these objections.

  - *If answers to Questions 5 and 6 are mixed,* this action is *moderately* ethical. Modify this decision in considerations of objections raised by Questions 5 or 6. You may need to further modify this decision in consideration of any "no" answer to Questions 2 through 4.

The six question framework can help managers reach a moral conclusion regarding the rightness or wrongness of any decision. The answers to Questions 5 and 6 point managers in the direction of the most moral decision. Doing something because the action is to the greatest good of the greatest number of people affected by it, and treats all stakeholders with respect and integrity, provides a tremendous amount of moral certitude. But if that action also might result in the decision-maker being fired (Question 2), more reflection might be needed to determine how to do what is right without being fired.

Note how the "legal" answer is not the highest ethical theory. Laws are not created out of thin air, they are justified by concerns about the greatest good for the greatest number and respect for everyone. Laws that fail to meet these two fundamental ethical concerns are usually an issue of public and political concern, debated, and sometimes changed.

The following sections describe the ethical foundation behind the questions that appear in Exhibit 5.1. Understanding the ethical foundation provides employees with greater confidence when applying the decision-making framework. In addition, the ethical theories enable employees to understand why they reach different moral conclusions for a particular decision.

The Five Ethical Theories

Questions 2 through 6 of the ethics decision-making framework each represent one of the five major ethical theories. The first question—"Who are all the people affected by the action?"—is referred to as stakeholder analysis and not considered an ethical theory. Identifying all the people affected by a decision helps to inform the ethical analysis.

The five ethical theories are ordered in Exhibit 5.2 beginning with the most basic and ending with the most important. Egoism (Question 2) is the most basic ethical theory; deontology is the most important and demanding ethical theory (Question 6). View these five ethical theories as sequential steps on a moral ladder, and the first step is egoism.

z

Five Ethical Theories

Egoism. How does the action relate to me? If the action furthers my interests, it is right. If it conflicts with my interests, it is wrong.

Social group relativism. How does the action relate to my social group (peers, friends, etc.)? If the action conforms with the social group's norms, it is right. If it is contrary to the social group's norms, it is wrong.

Cultural relativism. How does the action relate to the national culture, particularly its laws? If the action conforms with the law, it is right. If it is contrary to the law, it is wrong.

Utilitarianism. How does the action relate to everyone who is affected by it? If the action is beneficial to the greatest number of people affected by it, it is right. If it is detrimental to the greatest number, it is wrong.

Deontology. How does the action relate to my duty to become an ideal human being who treats others in the way that I would want to be treated? Does it treat *every stakeholder* truthfully and with respect and integrity? If it does, it is right. If it does not, it is wrong.

Egoism

When faced with a decision, an egoist asks: "How does the action relate to me? If the action conforms with my interests, it is right. If it conflicts with my interests, it is wrong." Egoists tend to reason as follows: "I strongly believe that *x* is the best decision, because that is my personal preference."

In *Theory of Moral Sentiments* and *Wealth of Nations*, Adam Smith emphasizes that people very naturally make economic decisions based on self-interest. Egoism is a morally acceptable ethical theory, as long as the pursuit of self-interest does not collapse into selfishness or generate harm.

Ayn Rand's novels *The Fountainhead* and *Atlas Shrugged* are among the most engaging articulations of the importance of egoism. Who we are, and what our interests are, matters a great deal. According to Rand, the best thing for the common good is to become an individual of high integrity willing to pursue one's self-interests at all costs.

Egoism as the predominant ethical theory, however, can be very problematic for organizations. In highly politicized organizations, individuals fight for scarce resources, such as office space or budgets, even though it is clearly more beneficial to the organization if one particular person received the scarce resource. If egoism is the predominant ethical theory, then the more politically powerful or astute employee gets the scarce resource, to the detriment of organizational performance.

Whose interests matter the most when two people have conflicting interests? Egoists seeking a reasonable solution to conflicts that arise between their interests and the interests of others will usually broaden their understanding to include the interests of larger social groups, thus taking the next step up the moral reasoning ladder.

Social Group Relativism

When faced with a decision, a social group relativist asks: "How does the action relate to my social group? If the action conforms with my social group's norms, it is right. If it is contrary to my social group's norms, it is wrong." Social group relativists tend to reason as follows: "I strongly believe that x is the best decision, because that is what my social group supports."

Associating oneself with the ethical standards of a group is often considered to be a higher stage of moral reasoning than egoism. Social group relativists are very concerned about what their social group (such as other managers, industry councils, and professional associations) thinks about an issue.

Social group relativism is a common ethical theory. Managers usually feel a strong affinity for the interests of other managers. When problems arise, a manager might ask other managers what they have done in the past when faced with a similar problem. The decision-maker wants to do what a good manager would do in the particular situation.

Similarly, nonmanagement employees usually feel a strong affinity for the interests of other nonmanagement employees, customers tend to view things from a customer's perspective, suppliers tend to view things from a supplier's perspective, and community members tend to view things from a community member's perspective.

Social group relativism as the predominant ethical theory, however, can be very problematic for organizations. In highly politicized organizations, departments fight for scarce resources even though it is clearly more beneficial to the organization if one particular department received the scarce resource. If social group relativism is the predominant ethical theory, then the more politically powerful or astute department or social group gets the scarce resource, to the detriment of organizational performance.

Which social group's interests matter the most when the two primary social groups involved in the situation have conflicting interests? Social group relativists seeking a reasonable solution to this dilemma will usually broaden their understanding to include the interests of the entire organization or larger society, thus taking the next step up the moral reasoning ladder.

Cultural Relativism

When faced with a decision a cultural relativist asks: "How does the action relate to my national culture, particularly the law? If the action conforms with the law, it is right. If it is contrary to the law, it is wrong." Cultural relativists tend to reason as follows: "I strongly believe that x is the right thing to do, because the law says so."

Associating oneself with the ethical standards embodied within a nation's laws is often considered to be a higher stage of moral reasoning than social group relativism. The person perceives herself or himself as a member of a larger society that has some common interests.

Cultural relativists are very concerned about what the legal system thinks about an issue. Laws are established through two distinct processes, Congress and the judicial system. Political legislation is the result of politicians presenting competing perspectives and reaching a conclusion by voting on the issue. Judicial laws are the result of lawyers presenting competing perspectives; a conclusion is reached by a judge hearing the case.

Cultural relativism is also a rather common ethical theory. Many managers do not want to break the law, even when doing so might personally benefit them or their company. When problems arise, they review the law, or ask company lawyers to provide them with a legal opinion. They want to do what is right in the eyes of the legal establishment.

Cultural relativism as the predominant ethical theory, however, can be very problematic for organizations. Sometimes laws conflict with one another, or following the law endangers the lives of others. Just because something is legal does not mean that it is ethical.

Cultural relativists seeking a reasonable solution to these dilemmas will usually broaden their understanding to include either determining the greatest good for the greatest number of people affected or individual rights, thus taking the next step up the moral reasoning ladder. These two highest theories are aimed at minimizing the most common human biases—a preference for our own interests, our social group's interests, or our culture's interests.

Utilitarianism

When faced with a decision, a utilitarian asks: "How does the action relate to everyone who is affected by it? If it is beneficial to the majority, then it is right. If it is detrimental to the majority of people, then it is wrong." Utilitarians tend to reason as follows: "I strongly believe that x is the best decision, because it benefits the greatest number of people."

Concern about an action's impact on the general welfare is often considered to be a higher stage of moral reasoning than cultural relativism. In this sense, the person is not just concerned about national laws, but whether the law is morally justified when the well-being of others are taken into consideration.

Utilitarians emphasize the consequences of an action on all those affected by it. The ethics of capitalism is based on utilitarian logic—the economic pursuit of self-interest improves national wealth more than other economic systems.

Everyone counts equally under utilitarianism. There can be no favoritism based on status or power. Utilitarian-thinking managers would centrally locate a scarce piece of equipment needed by everyone, rather than give preference to the employee or department with the most political power. Whatever is best for the organization determines the action taken.

How can a manager know what is best for everyone? One formal method is to allow each affected person to vote his or her preference. Democracy is utilitarian in the sense that everyone's vote counts equally. Following an unresolved contentious debate at a management meeting, someone might suggest that a binding vote be taken. The outcome of the vote is considered legitimate because it expresses the will of the majority.

In 1996, Ken Lay applied utilitarian logic, as well as the other ethical theories, to determine who should be Enron's new chief operating officer (COO), the person who would eventually succeed him as Enron's future CEO (see *In the Real World: Transferring Managerial Power—1996*). This person would need to please multiple stakeholder groups by inspiring employees and stockholders and appropriately managing customer, supplier, and government relations.

IN THE REAL WORLD

Transferring Managerial Power—1996

Investment bankers participated in Andy Fastow's SPE arrangements, and Enron reported record revenue and profit levels. With the help of mergers and acquisitions, Enron became the world's largest natural gas company, and its stock price continued to perform well. In 1996, *Fortune* magazine named Enron "America's Most Innovative Company."

Ken Lay, having saved the company, was now ready to train his successor. Enron's future CEO would first have to learn how to manage the Fortune 100 firm's day-to-day operations as Chief Operating Officer (COO). Lay's plan called for the COO to be promoted to CEO by 2001.

The three internal candidates for COO were the CEO of Enron's traditional natural gas pipeline division, the CEO of the highly successful Gas Bank division (Jeff Skilling), and the CEO of the growing international business division. A fourth possibility was to hire a highly qualified outsider.

Skilling strongly advocated for the position and threatened to quit if not promoted to COO. Skilling accused the international division's CEO of mismanagement and incompetence. He also opposed the natural gas pipeline division CEO, arguing that the new economy valued intellectual skills and market transactions more highly than traditional brick-and-mortar assets. Only he, Skilling argued, possessed the appropriate vision for Enron.

Meanwhile, Skilling's weaknesses included a lack of hands-on cash management experience, taking extreme risks, impatience with those who did not quickly grasp his intellectual and visionary insights, competitiveness with other executives, and arrogance.

DECISION CHOICE. If you were the CEO of Enron, who would you promote to COO:

❶ The CEO of the traditional natural gas pipeline division?

❷ Jeff Skilling, the CEO of the highly successful Gas Bank division?

❸ The CEO of the growing international division?

❹ A highly qualified outsider?

Why?

Utilitarianism as the predominant ethical theory, however, can be very problematic for organizations. Managers of an organization composed of white males might decide that the organization would perform with optimal harmony if it did not employ any women or African-Americans. Or, managers might decide not to install pollution prevention devices that would only benefit a few people living near the facility.

Utilitarians seeking a reasonable solution to these issues will usually broaden their understanding to include human rights, thus taking the final step up the moral reasoning ladder.

Deontology

When faced with a decision, a deontologist asks: "How does the action relate to my duty to treat others in the way that I would want to be treated? Does it treat every person truthfully and with integrity? If it does, then it is right. If it does not, then it is wrong." Deontologists tend to reason as follows: "I strongly believe that x is the best decision, because we have a duty to treat everyone with respect."

Respecting all stakeholders is often considered the highest stage of moral reasoning. In this sense, the individual is not just concerned about the will of the majority, but whether each and every person is treated fairly.

Deontologists emphasize the motives behind an action and individual rights, rather than consequences. They follow "moral rules," such as the Ten Commandments and the Golden Rule, "do unto others as you would want done to you." People who want others to respect them have a duty to respect others. For a deontologist, the appropriate action is to *always* be honest, keep promises, provide mutual aid when needed, and respect people and property. Deontologists want to embody the moral qualities of a saint.

Deontology gives managers the most difficult moral problems, because the ethical theory demands that the organization respect every stakeholder all the time in its pursuit of revenue or profits.

Wal-Mart's recent evolution is a classic case of deontology's power. Wal-Mart achieved the lowest prices and high corporate profits by paying employees below living wages and denying them affordable healthcare coverage. In response to the negative publicity caused by media exposes and social justice activists, Wal-Mart improved employee wages and health benefits.

Although deontology is considered the most important ethical theory, it too can be very problematic if considered in isolation from the four ethical theories on the lower rungs of the moral reasoning ladder. Focusing solely on respecting the interests of every stakeholder is not always achievable, practical, or desirable.

Assume that given time and budget limitations, employees must choose whether to provide preferential service to the largest revenue-generating customer or give all customers an equal amount of inadequate service. The 80/20 Rule suggests that 20% of an organization's customer base provides 80% of its revenue.[4] If the top revenue-generating customers are not satisfied, they might take their business elsewhere, which could bankrupt the organization.

Deontologists seeking a reasonable solution to these issues will usually broaden their understanding to include general welfare calculations, legal concerns, social group-interests, and self-interests.

Both utilitarianism and deontology matter a great deal. In many situations, the two highest ethical theories arrive at similar conclusions, providing the decision-maker with a tremendous amount of moral certitude. Sometimes they may conflict. When this happens, respecting everyone is considered the most important ethical response. When this is not a practical solution, serving the greatest good or one of the other ethical theories takes on greater moral weight.

Persuading Others

After applying the ethical decision-making framework, two employees may still sincerely disagree about what is the ethically correct action to take. Most managers are primarily social group relativists (Question 3) and concerned about the law (Question 4). Other managers may be primarily egoists (Question 2), utilitarians (Question 5), or deontologists (Question 6).

When this happens in organizations, the person with higher status tends to get his or her way. This conflict resolution approach assumes that the higher status person is, by default, more ethical, an assumption that has been proven false innumerable times in human history. This conflict resolution approach also damages employee morale and can result in unethical behaviors and lawsuits.

A healthier approach is for people to listen carefully to each other, categorize the other person's response in terms of one of the five ethical theories, and then reframe the analysis using the other person's ethical theory.

Each ethical theory is like a different foreign language. Egoism (self-interests) is equivalent to speaking English while Utilitarianism (greatest good) is equivalent to Spanish. If an English speaker wants to persuade a Spanish speaker, the English speaker must communicate in Spanish, otherwise no progress will be made. The same logic applies to the use of ethical theories.

Assume that an egoist believes the right thing to do is x, a utilitarian believes the right thing is y, and the egoist wants to persuade the utilitarian. Utilitarians do not care what is in their self-interest, so appealing to a utilitarian's self-interest will fall on deaf ears. What utilitarians do care about is the greatest good for the greatest number of people. To be persuasive, the egoist must communicate using utilitarian reasoning and demonstrate how a greatest good analysis results in doing x rather than y.

Similarly, egoists do not care about the greatest good for the greatest number of people, so appealing to an egoist's sense of the greatest good will fall on deaf ears. What egoists do care about is their self-interests. To be persuasive, the utilitarian must communicate using egoistic reasoning and demonstrate how it is in the individual's self-interest to do y rather than x.

After hearing all of these different perspectives, consensus still might not be achieved, and the decision-maker has to reach a decision unilaterally. By going through this process, the decision maker is able to justify the decision based on all of the competing ethical theories. The other employees may not agree with the manager's final conclusion, but they will understand the manager's ethical reasoning, and be able to convey that reasoning to other organizational members.

TIPS AND TECHNIQUES

Achieving Ethical Consensus

Many ethical disagreements can be solved. Use the following steps to help people achieve ethical consensus and win-win ethical outcomes.[5]

Step 1. Both parties state their position on the issue.

Step 2. Both parties reveal the values that underlie their position.

Step 3. Both parties paraphrase each other's position.

Step 4. Both parties paraphrase each other's underlying values.

Step 5. Both parties, working together, craft a resolution to the conflict over the issue.

Step 6. Both parties check that the resolution does not conflict with their own values or the values of the other party.

Ten "Ethical Hazard Approaching" Signs

Employees in a manufacturing facility with toxic chemicals are visually warned when entering hazardous areas by flashing red lights, loud sirens, and large signs with skulls and crossbones. Unfortunately, warning lights do not flash when employees enter an ethical hazard zone.

Michael Josephson describes 10 common rationalizations for unethical acts.[6] Pause and reflect on the thought, "It's ethical because it's legal." Ethics is more than just the law. Laws change all the time, often because an individual, or group of people, strongly believes that an existing law, such as slavery in the 19th century, is unethical.

Josephson's ten rationalizations are presented as "ethical hazard approaching" signs in Exhibit 5.3. Employees must be trained to recognize these rationalizations and then apply the systematic ethical decision-making framework to determine a moral answer.

EXHIBIT 5.3

Ten "Ethical Hazard Approaching" Signs

Beware When Someone Says:

1. It's ethical . . . if it's legal and permissible.
2. It's ethical . . . if it's necessary.
3. It's ethical . . . if it's just part of the job.
4. It's ethical . . . if it's all for a good cause.
5. It's ethical . . . if I'm just doing it for you.
6. It's ethical . . . if I'm just fighting fire with fire.
7. It's ethical . . . if it doesn't hurt anyone.
8. It's ethical . . . if everyone else is doing it.
9. It's ethical . . . if I don't gain personally.
10. It's ethical . . . if I've got it coming.

Summary

This chapter provides a systemic ethics decision-making framework for deriving moral conclusions to business problems. The framework takes into consideration the perspectives of five major ethical theories and rank-orders their concerns in a useful manner. Using this framework helps employees understand the ethical ramifications of business issues.

Notes

1. www.rotary.org, accessed 9/08/08.
2. Dayton Fandray, "The Ethical Company," *Workforce*, 79, no. 12 (2000): 74–78, available at www.raytheon.com/stewardship/ethics/index.html, accessed 9/08/08.
3. Denis Collins and Laura Page, "A Socrates/Ted Koppel Paradigm for Integrating the Teaching of Business Ethics in the Curriculum," in Sandra Waddock, ed., *Research in Corporate Social Performance and Policy*, 15, Supplement 2, special issue on "Teaching Business and Society Courses with Reflective and Active Learning Strategies" (Greenwich, CT: JAI Press, 1997): 221–242.
4. Richard Koch, *The 80/20 Principle* (New York: Currency Books, 1999).
5. Warren French, "Business Ethics Training: Face-to-Face and at a Distance," *Journal of Business Ethics*, 66, no. 1 (2006): 117–126.
6. http://josephsoninstitute.org/business/overview/faq.html#10, accessed 8/15/08.

CHAPTER 6

Ethics Training

After reading this chapter, you will be able to:

- Describe the extent of ethics training nationwide
- Understand the shortcomings of Web-based ethics training programs
- Conduct ten types of ethics training workshops
- Develop business ethics scenarios for workshop discussion
- Administer personality surveys that measure character attributes associated with ethical behavior
- Assess the ethics training workshop

Individuals are more likely to discuss work-related ethical issues with family and friends than coworkers or executives. Ethics training initiates dialogue at work around contentious ethical issues and has greater impact on employee behaviors than the presence of an ethics code or memos from the boss. Ethics training helps to create a culture of trust. People employed in organizations with formalized ethics training have more positive perceptions about their organization's ethics and greater job satisfaction.[1]

This chapter reviews the extent of ethics training nationwide, recommends that ethics training include everyone in the organization, and highlights problems with Web-based ethics training programs. Ten different types of ethics training workshops that have received very favorable responses from managers and employees are presented for immediate implementation.

Extent of Ethics Training

A 2004 survey of publicly traded companies found that 68% provided ethics training.[2] City governments are more diligent than corporations in this matter, with more than 80% providing ethics training for employees.[3]

Ethics training is also required by some professions. Many states mandate that continuing education courses for accountants and lawyers include an ethics component.[4] All members of the National Association of Realtors® must complete ethics training courses.[5] Professional organizations, such as the AICPA, provide ethics resources on their Web sites, including a list of disciplinary actions.[6]

Organizations may be tempted to eliminate ethics training as an extraneous expense when budgets are tight, but this is exactly when ethics training is needed most. Remind employees, particularly those who tend toward relativism, that cutting ethical corners to "save the organization" might sound heroic in the short-term, but can come back to haunt the organization in the long-term.

Who to Train

Ethics training should be conducted throughout the organization. All employees, ranging from the CEO and Board of Directors to the janitor, experience ethical dilemmas on a daily basis. In 2000, shortly after officially adopting a Code of Ethics, Best Buy provided ethics training for all of its 140,000 employees in the United States and Canada.[7]

Enron and other scandals highlight the importance of ethics training at the highest level of the organization. Although ethics training is important to all constituents, middle managers deserve special attention. They are stuck in a difficult position, responsible for implementing the desires of corporate executives on a day-to-day basis yet fully aware of the organization's limited resources—and among the first to be informed about unethical behaviors.

Both new and long-term employees need ethics training. Making ethics training part of a new employee's orientation process demonstrates the importance of ethics to the organization. Conduct a follow-up session six months later to reinforce the importance of ethics and explore ethical issues they have experienced at work up to that point.

Long-term employees significantly shape the organization's ethical tone. One long-term employee denigrating the organization's ethical efforts can undo all the managerial effort put into aligning a new employee with the organization's ethics. Train long-term employees to lead ethics training sessions and share stories on how the organization's code of ethics was upheld in difficult situations.

Web-Based Ethics Training

According to one survey, companies conduct more than 90% of their ethics training through e-learning programs.[8] Online versions are easy to implement. At Coors, new hires are required to complete the Web-based training module within 90 days.[9]

Internet ethics training programs should supplement, not replace, the most effective ethics training method—facilitator-guided face-to-face interactions and group activities. Ethics training requires dialogue. The best response to even the most cut-and-dried ethical dilemma can be highly debatable, but you can't argue with a computer program.

Another inadequacy of Web-based training is that employees are not pushed out of their ethics comfort zone. Skilled facilitators can guide the discussion to other relevant issues worthy of exploration, point out contradictions, and call on quiet participants to express their views in a safe learning environment. Interactive training workshops can also enhance team building and collegiality.

Facilitating an Ethics Discussion

Create a safe learning environment by choosing someone the participants trust to facilitate the ethics training workshop. The responsibility should be assigned to a trustworthy human resources department staff person who has a solid understanding of human resource issues. But some employees will not speak honestly in front of a human resources employee, particularly about ethical issues, because they fear being fired or that their comments will have a negative impact on performance evaluations.

If this is the case, assign the facilitator role to someone both the boss and employees trust. The person can be an informal leader from within the work unit, someone everyone respects who works in another department, or an outside consultant. The best option is to train an informal leader from within the work unit who has management potential. This person already has a good feel for some of the key ethical issues and can make sure the discussion is realistic and relevant.

A good facilitator inspires self-learning among the participants by keeping everyone focused on the main issues while being flexible to new issues as they arise. The facilitator should encourage participants to analyze and modify their own views.

Ethics Training Options

Exhibit 6.1 lists a wide variety of ethics training workshop options. Each training option will be discussed in greater detail.

EXHIBIT 6.1

Ethics Training Workshop Options

1. *Code of Ethics assessment.* Review the Code of Ethics. Have employees assess how well the organization is living up to the code, praise areas of strength, and develop strategies for improving the lowest scoring areas.

2. *Code of Conduct content.* Create a *Who Wants to be a Millionaire* or *Jeopardy* quiz show asking questions about the organization's Code of Conduct.

3. *Code of Conduct violations and outcomes.* Present actual cases of employees, or people in the industry, violating a code of conduct, and the punishments they received.

(Continued)

EXHIBIT 6.1

(Continued)

4. *Applying the Code to specific situations.* Provide several real-life situations and have participants determine whether the behavior is in accordance with, or violates, the Code of Conduct.

5. *Creating business ethics scenarios for discussion.* Have employees create ethical scenarios based on their own experiences and discuss them.

6. *Applying the ethics decision-making framework.* Teach participants the six-question Ethical Decision-Making Framework, provide several real-life situations, and have them use the framework to derive a moral solution to the situation.

7. *"Ethical hazard approaching."* Review a list of common rationalizations for unethical behavior, discuss situations when these reasons have been given to justify behaviors, and then brainstorm a more ethical response in case a similar situation arises in the future.

8. *Personality analysis.* Administer surveys that measure character attributes associated with ethical or unethical behavior, such as conscientiousness, organizational citizenship behavior, social dominance orientation, locus of control, Machiavellianism, and individualism/collectivism.

9. *Ideal employee expectations.* Develop a profile of an "ideal employee," put the profile into a survey format, have employees assess themselves to this ideal, praise the good, analyze shortcomings, and develop strategies for transforming weaknesses into strengths.

10. *Work as a calling.* Reflect on making job tasks enjoyable and meaningful experiences.

Code of Ethics Assessment Training

Employees should annually assess the organization's ethical perform-ance based on its Code of Ethics. If an organization has the time and financial resources to conduct only one ethics workshop a year, this should be it. A nine-step process for conducting this workshop appears in Exhibit 4.2 (see Chapter 4).

Code of Conduct Content Training

A Code of Conduct can be long and complicated. Enron's Code of Ethics fit on a business card, but its Code of Conduct exceeded 60 pages.[10] Use a game format to engage the minds of employees when educating them about the Code of Conduct's content. *Jeopardy* and *Who Wants to Be a Millionaire* offer two television game formats that are a fun way to raise awareness.

In *Jeopardy*, three contestants compete to be the first person to provide the correct response.[11] The game board consists of six col-umns, each representing a different topic. The five rows contain answers that escalate in difficulty and monetary value. If the contestant provides the wrong question, the monetary amount is deducted from previous winnings. Whoever has the highest monetary earnings at the end of the game wins a prize. In this modified version of *Jeopardy*, insert questions at the intersection of each row and column and chal-lenge the contestants to be the first one to provide the correct answer. Allow workshop participants time to discuss each answer as needed.

In *Who Wants to Be a Millionaire*, teams of workshop partici-pants compete to answer successively difficult questions.[12] The questions could be either "fill in the blank" or multiple choice, such as:

Who is the organization's Ethics Officer?

The next round could be about the law:

Which one of the following is an appropriate reason for rejecting a job applicant: A) age, B) religion, C) gender, D) physical disability, or E) inability to perform the required task?

Code of Conduct Violations and Outcomes Training

Many employees cynically believe that criminals are neither caught nor punished. But in reality, crime does not pay. Design a workshop educating employees about the types of unethical activities that have previously occurred within the organization or industry, and how the guilty person was punished.

The U.S. Department of Defense maintains an ongoing list of ethical violations and corresponding punishments for use in an ethics training program.[13] A short description of the unethical behavior is followed by the specific code being violated and the assessed punishment. Categories in the September 2007 report include abuse of position, bribery, credit card abuse, fraud, gifts, travel violations, and misuse of government resources and personnel.

Reading these scenarios enables employees to realize that individuals are not only caught for code violations, but also severely disciplined. The crimes, and corresponding punishments, include:

EXHIBIT 6.2

"Match the Bribe to the Penalty" Exercise

Instructions: Match the bribery code violation with the jail sentence.

1. Employee recommended a contractor who charged inflated prices in exchange for $115,000.

   A. 4 months in jail

2. Employee approved supplier contract in exchange for laptop computer.

   B. 7 months in jail

3. Employee enrolled Korean pilots into a flight school in exchange for a paid trip to Korea.

   C. 46 months in jail

Correct Answers: 1-C, 2-B, 3-A

- Authorized purchase of non-work related clothing: Reassigned

- Showed police government ID to avoid ticket: Demoted

- Romantic relationship with government contractor: Reassigned

- Obtained free auto repairs from supplier: Fired

This information can be delivered in an engaging manner, as shown in Exhibit 6.2.

Applying the Code of Conduct to Specific Situations Training

Coca-Cola's ethics training includes reviewing the company's Code of Business Conduct and determining whether several real-life scenarios are in accordance with, or violate, the code.[14] Employees doing this exercise realize the complexity, difficulty, and necessity of applying the code.

Coca-Cola's Code of Business Conduct appears in Exhibit 6.3, along with a scenario and correct answer. The employee learns about previous disciplinary actions taken by the organization. These types of training activities reinforce the serious ramifications of unethical behaviors.

EXHIBIT 6.3

Coca-Cola's Code of Business Conduct Exercise

OUR PROMISE
The Coca-Cola Company
exists to benefit and
refresh everyone it touches.

YOUR COMMITMENT
As a representative of
The Coca-Cola Company,
you must act with honesty and
integrity in all matters.

- Employees must follow the law wherever they are around the world.

- Employees must avoid conflicts of interest. Be aware of appearances.

- Financial records—both for internal activities and external transactions—must be timely and accurate.

- Company assets—including computers, materials, and work time—must not be used for personal benefit.

- Customers and suppliers must be dealt with fairly and at arm's length.

- Employees must never attempt to bribe or improperly influence a government official.

- Employees must safeguard the company's nonpublic information.

- Violations of the Code include asking other employees to violate the Code, not reporting a Code violation, or failing to cooperate in a Code investigation.

- Violating the Code will result in discipline. Discipline will vary depending on the circumstances and may include, alone or in combination, a letter of reprimand, demotion, loss of merit increase, bonus or stock options, suspension, or even termination.

- Under the Code, certain actions require written approval by your Principal Manager.

If you have questions about any situation, ask. Always ask.

Scenario: An administrative assistant's husband owns an office supply firm with lower prices than anyone else. The assistant's duties at the company include ordering office supplies, so she ordered them from her husband's firm. Does this violate the code?
Answer: Yes, this is a conflict of interest. A Principal Manager must approve in advance any transaction in which an employee has a financial interest. The employee was disciplined.

Creating Business Ethics Scenarios for Discussion Training

The most meaningful ethical issues to explore are those employees observe, experience, or hear about while employed either in their current organization or for a previous employer. Employees should develop written scenarios about these ethical issues and share them with others.

Limit the write-up to one page, and the decision options to two or three responses. Otherwise, the ensuing discussion will be difficult to manage. This workshop can also serve as a team-building activity.

Exhibit 6.4 provides instructions for writing an ethical dilemma narrative.

EXHIBIT 6.4

Ethical Dilemma Narrative Exercise

As employees, you have experienced or observed many ethical dilemmas. Write a *one- or two-paragraph* ethical dilemma about an experience that challenged your understanding of business ethics. Three ways that might help you arrive at an issue are:

1. Describe an incident at work that challenged your conscience.
2. Describe an incident at work that challenged the organization's Code of Ethics or Code of Conduct.
3. Describe an incident that seemed disrespectful toward owners, customers, managers, employees, suppliers, community, or the natural environment.

To preserve anonymity, *change references to specific people and places.*

- Begin the first sentence with: "You are the (state the job title of the key person facing the ethical dilemma e.g., the accounting manager)."
- Describe the dilemma (context, concerns, conflict) and clarify both sides of the issue (other people need to understand why the unethical option was a reasonable thing for the decision-maker to pursue).

- Reach the key decision point, and then ask, "What would you do?" followed by several possible action options, such as (1) Inform *x* or (2) Do nothing.

  You will then read your dilemma in a small group and ask others what action option they would pursue if they were the decision-maker facing the dilemma.

The workshop facilitator can provide an example of an ethical dilemma narrative to help participants with the writing process. The example distributed should contain an ethical lesson the manager wants the workshop participants to learn. The "Sick Leave?" scenario in Exhibit 6.5 is worthwhile because it represents an issue common across industries.

Emphasize the importance of anonymity when writing the dilemma. The point of writing the dilemma is to highlight, for the sake of public discussion, difficult issues that arise at work, rather than to embarrass anyone.

Put the employees in small groups of three or four to discuss the written dilemma. Each person should read his or her written dilemma and then have the other group members choose a decision option. The employee who wrote the dilemma should clarify issues and facilitate the small group discussion. The group should choose one of its dilemmas to share with the entire workshop. The group should rewrite the dilemma to more clearly describe the situation and add explanations so only two or three options are available to the decision-maker.

These scenarios can be used in a follow-up ethics training workshop that teaches employees how to apply the ethics decision-making framework. They can also be used by the human resources

EXHIBIT 6.5

"Sick Leave?" Ethical Dilemma Narrative

You supervise 10 employees. Kim, the best performer, called in sick today. You learn from a very trustworthy subordinate that Kim is not actually sick. Instead, Kim is taking a "mental health" day and just wanted some unscheduled time off from work. The company's sick leave policy does not allow for mental health days. You suspect that Kim might do this once or twice a year, within the allowable sick day allocation. Allowing Kim to take a "mental health" day off when not sick can damage employee morale by creating a double standard, one for Kim and one for everyone else. What would you do? Would you:

1. Demand that Kim work an extra day without pay to make up for the missed work day?

2. Just give Kim a warning?

3. Do nothing?

Why?

department as part of the interview process to determine the ethics of potential job candidates (see Chapter 3).

Applying the Ethics Decision-Making Framework Training

This training workshop teaches employees how to apply the ethics decision-making framework to particular situations. The six-step facilitation process in Exhibit 6.6 is aimed at maximizing interactive dialogue.

EXHIBIT 6.6

Facilitating an Ethics Dialogue Workshop

Step 1. Distribute the six-question ethics decision-making framework and review it using a sample business problem.

Step 2. Distribute a real-life situation to workshop participants, read it out loud, and have participants apply the ethics decision-making framework to derive a moral conclusion that supports one of the decision options.

Step 3. Count the votes for each recommendation.

Step 4. Develop position rationale in small groups.

Step 5. Empower the minority position.

Step 6. Reach a conclusion.

Distribute the ethics decision-making framework (see Exhibit 5.1 in Chapter 5) and read the instructions for using the framework. Go over a short case, such as the "Sick Time" dilemma presented in Exhibit 6.5, to demonstrate how to apply the questions and evaluate the alternatives.

Distribute the real-life situation as a handout and read it out loud. Some participants will want to choose a response that is not provided. For the sake of conciseness, provide a reason why the newly proposed option is not possible. Have the workshop participants write answers to the six ethics decision-making framework questions, circle the decision option that they would choose, and

Requiring Written Response to Ethical Dilemmas

A written answer to an ethical dilemma typically fosters greater reflection than simply stating a verbal opinion. A written answer:

- Commits the person to a particular decision option

- Prevents employees from changing their decision based on how others vote

- Provides the facilitator with a hook to involve a quiet participant ("Could you please read your written answer to the workshop?")

- Provides an initial data point that can be compared to an employee's belief at the end of the workshop

then write one sentence describing why that option is the best answer. People can agree on the same option, yet disagree as to why that is the right choice. With ethics, why an option is chosen is more revealing than which action is chosen.

Write on the board how many employees voted for each decision option. By publicly tallying the votes, employees quickly learn that not everyone agrees with them. An evenly divided vote is a sign of a well-written business problem.

Next, put workshop attendees on teams based on common responses. Enhance the learning experience by forming teams no smaller than three, and no larger than five, employees. If six people choose the same option, divide them into two teams of three employees each.

Have each person read his or her one-sentence "Why?" answer to the other team members. If different justifications are provided, have the team prioritize them. Then have the team discuss why the options chosen by the other teams are less desirable. Assign one team member the role of devil's advocate who argues on behalf of the other options. This enables the team to develop more thoughtful responses as to what is wrong with the opposing views.

Choose the team with the minority viewpoint to come to the front of the workshop and present its perspective. The team holding the minority view should always speak first. If a team with the majority opinion speaks first, those holding a minority view may be so overwhelmed that they do not want to express a contrary opinion, particularly if members of the majority view team have institutional authority. If workshop teams are evenly divided among the available options, any team can present first.

Then have participants go back into their respective teams and develop an answer that addresses all of the concerns expressed. The team can develop a win-win situation that integrates all views expressed, or choose one option over another, but this time with a more thorough understanding and response to the opposing perspective. Choose one team to share its final decision and poll the other workshop participants to see how many agree.

In the Real World: SPE Investments—1997 provides an ethical dilemma that can be used during this workshop. Have the participants apply the six ethical decision-making framework questions to Michael Kopper's problem at Enron. If they conclude that Kopper should refuse to participate in his boss's plan, then question attendees as to whether Kopper should notify the CEO, the auditors, and/or the SEC.

SPE Investments—1997

Ken Lay decided to promote Jeff Skilling to COO, beginning in March 1997. Skilling quickly began planning to succeed Lay as CEO in 2001. With his power extended to other divisions, Skilling inserted loyalists in key executive positions throughout Enron.

Skilling promoted Andy Fastow to Vice-President of Treasury and Business Funding, with a goal of raising $20 billion a year in capital. Everyone needing capital would have to cooperate with Fastow's group. If they didn't, Fastow reminded them, he could ruin their careers.

During 1997, Enron still had too much debt on its books and needed cash. Fastow created a new SPE called RADR. The SPE would borrow money to pay Enron $17 million cash for an ownership stake in one of Enron's wind farms. This sale would remove the wind farm's debt from Enron's balance sheet.

Outside investors had profited nicely in Fastow-structured SPEs. Fastow now wanted to invest in the RADR SPE so he could profit too. Enron's Code of Conduct, however, prohibited senior executives from having a financial stake in any organization doing business with Enron. Such business transactions would create a major conflict of interest—would the executive be more concerned about Enron's economic interests or the other business's economic interest?

Fastow approached Michael Kopper, his assistant and protégé, with a way to get around this legally binding stipulation. Fastow's wife could loan Kopper $419,000 and he could give this money to his domestic partner to create an investment group called "Friends of Enron," which could then invest in RADR as the independent outside third party. Kopper, in turn, could pay back the loan, and distribute RADR profits, to the Fastows.

Kopper could write multiple "gift" checks to Fastow family members below the minimum amount required to be reported to the IRS for tax purposes, and to the Fastow Foundation, a tax-exempt Houston charitable organization created by Andy.

DECISION CHOICE. If your boss, an Enron Vice President, instructed you to participate in this plan, would you:

1 Support the plan?

2 Risk getting fired for refusing to participate in the plan?

3 Inform CEO Ken Lay about the plan?

4 Notify Arthur Andersen auditors about the plan?

5 Notify the SEC about the plan?

Why?

"Ethical Hazard Approaching" Training

Michael Josephson highlights 10 common rationalizations that, when spoken, should raise employee awareness an ethical hazard is approaching (see Exhibit 5.3 in Chapter 5). Read the list and after each rationalization ask participants to share stories about when they heard this rationalization given. Then have attendees propose a more ethical course of action for this situation.

Personality Analysis Training

Ethics training can help participants better understand the ethical implications of their own personality styles. A host of personality surveys provide useful information, including conscientiousness, organizational citizenship behavior, social dominance orientation, locus of control, and Machiavellianism.

Chapter 3 summarizes several psychological scales that measure a person's ethical tendencies: conscientiousness, organizational citizenship behavior, and social dominance orientation. These personality surveys can be administered during a workshop for the purpose of self-understanding and improvement.

Locus of Control

Locus of control refers to whether individuals believe they control the events in their lives (internal locus of control), or the events in their lives are the result of things beyond their control (external locus of control).[15] Locus of control survey scales are widely available.[16]

Researchers have found a relationship between locus of control and ethical behavior.[17] People with a strong internal locus of control exhibit more ethical behavior than those with a strong external locus of control. Research has also shown that people with a strong internal locus of control are better able to resist coercion, thus less susceptible to pressure from unethical bullies.

Machiavellianism

Some unethical activities at work are the result of "the ends justify the means" moral thinking. Individuals may behave unethically to achieve a highly desired future outcome.

This type of ethical theorizing is known as Machiavellianism. Many Machiavellians have a "do whatever it takes" attitude toward goal accomplishment. For instance, a Machiavellian might intentionally lie about anticipated workforce layoffs next month to get the most productivity out of subordinates prior to the formal announcement.

There is a good side to Machiavellianism. Machiavellians are very determined, goal-oriented people. Provide Machiavellians with a difficult objective and they may develop several creative strategies that a deontologist might not have considered for moral reasons.

A survey instrument has been developed to measure a person's Machiavellian propensity.[18] "High Mach" employees deserve a manager's special attention. Someone reporting that she or he believes "the best way to handle people is to tell them what they want to hear" can cause significant organizational problems due to misinformation. Managers should allow Machiavellians the liberty to pursue their interests as long as they do not violate the organization's Code of Ethics or Conduct of Conduct.

Ideal Employee Expectations Training

Employees need to know in advance what managers expect of them. Managers usually have an image about how an ideal subordinate behaves, and this might not match the image subordinates possess.

Restrict the first workshop to managers. Ask them to list the behavioral attributes of an ideal employee, such as keeping promises or continually learning best practices. Share these lists in small groups and combine similar items under the same heading, such as customer relations. Next each manager should choose the categories and behavioral items that are most relevant to his or her work unit.

The second workshop on this topic should be restricted to subordinates. Present the composite profile of an ideal employee for the purposes of feedback. Are these behavior items reasonable expectations? Any changes employees suggest should be presented to the manager for consideration.

Then transform the ideal employee profile into a survey instrument for self-assessment purposes. Have participants benchmark themselves to the ideal employee, praise the good, analyze shortcomings, and develop strategies for transforming weaknesses into strengths. This can be done individually or as a small group activity with constructive feedback and suggestions. The ideal employee profile should be part of the annual performance appraisal analysis.

Exhibit 6.7 provides an example of an ideal employee self-assessment survey.[19]

EXHIBIT 6.7

Qualities of an Ideal Employee: Self-Assessment Survey

Instructions: Please use the 1–5 scale below to assess how well each of the following statements exemplifies your work performance. The more honest you are, the more helpful the information you will receive.

1=*Strongly Disagree*; 2=*Disagree*; 3=*Neither Agree nor Disagree*; 4=*Agree*; 5=*Strongly Agree*

	SD	D	N	A	SA
General Character					
I treat all employees, agents, and other business contacts with respect.	1	2	3	4	5
I keep my promises.	1	2	3	4	5
I hold myself accountable for my actions.	1	2	3	4	5
I abide by organizational policies and procedures.	1	2	3	4	5

General Character Subtotal: Add the four scores and divide by four:					
Customer Relations					
I know what my customers need and expect.	1	2	3	4	5
I have rapport with my customers.	1	2	3	4	5
I understand and meet service expectations.	1	2	3	4	5
I inform customers when I am not available, when I will return, and to whom their communications can be directed in my absence.	1	2	3	4	5
Customer Relations Subtotal: Add the four scores and divide by four:					
Colleague Relations					
I am an active member of my team.	1	2	3	4	5
I provide constructive criticism.	1	2	3	4	5
I learn best practices from other employees.	1	2	3	4	5
I help other employees.	1	2	3	4	5
Colleague Relations Subtotal: Add the four scores and divide by four:					
Communication Skills					
I listen actively by providing appropriate and timely responses.	1	2	3	4	5
I keep written communications concise and grammatically correct.	1	2	3	4	5
I date correspondence and include my name and contact points.	1	2	3	4	5

(Continued)

EXHIBIT 6.7

(Continued)

I return telephone messages on the day they are received.	1	2	3	4	5
I use the most effective form of communication for specific situations.	1	2	3	4	5

Communication Skills Subtotal:
Add the five scores and divide by five:

Work Task Skills

I do my assigned work.	1	2	3	4	5
I organize my work and work space for efficient use of my time.	1	2	3	4	5
I ask my colleagues for help when I need it.	1	2	3	4	5
I am responsive to questions about my work.	1	2	3	4	5
I ask for, and use, feedback.	1	2	3	4	5

Work Task Skills Subtotal:
Add the five scores and divide by five:

Continuous Improvement

I am receptive to change.	1	2	3	4	5
I identify opportunities to improve my job.	1	2	3	4	5
I incorporate improvements into my daily work.	1	2	3	4	5
I communication and collaborate with my team to implement improvements.	1	2	3	4	5
I disagree when it is likely to promote constructive change.	1	2	3	4	5

I set objectives to enhance my professional growth.	1	2	3	4	5
I enroll and actively participate in professional development opportunities.	1	2	3	4	5
I am prepared to explain how I contribute to the organization.	1	2	3	4	5
Continuous Improvement Skills Subtotal: *Add the eight scores and divide by eight:*					
Company Pride					
I actively promote the accomplishments of the organization.	1	2	3	4	5
I celebrate my successes and those of the organization.	1	2	3	4	5
I volunteer and participate annually in at least one organization activity, function, group outing, etc., that is not directly related to my job.	1	2	3	4	5
I volunteer annually for at least one community activity.	1	2	3	4	5
Company Pride Skills Subtotal: *Add the four scores and divide by four:*					

Work as a Calling

Every job task can be a very meaningful experience and every employee can bring joy into the lives of others.[20] Employees should exhibit passion for their daily work activities and pride in their accomplishments.

All jobs can be a calling or vocation. Some people may feel called to market products that improve a customer's quality of life, others may feel called to be administrative assistants whose service improves the work unit's performance. No matter what the job task, the end result can be meaningful interactions with customers or coworkers. Contributing to the development of a high integrity organization with superior performance is a very meaningful activity.

In a workshop setting, have employees individually answer the sets of questions in Exhibit 6.8 and discuss their responses in small groups. These discussions can either help employees see their daily

EXHIBIT 6.8

Work as a Calling

When did you first feel drawn to the kind of work you are doing?

- What did it feel like?
- Has this feeling increased or decreased over the years?
- How can this feeling be regenerated?

Do you experience joy in your work?

- When and under what circumstances?
- How often do you experience this?
- How does this joy relate to difficulties associated with your work?

Do others experience joy as a result of your work?

- Directly?
- Indirectly?
- How can this experience of joy be increased?

What do you learn at work?

- In what ways is work a learning experience for you?
- In what ways is work a learning experience for others?

How is your work a blessing to future generations?

If you were to quit work today, what difference would it make to:

- Your personal or spiritual growth?
- The personal or spiritual growth of your work colleagues?

job tasks as something that can have a positive impact on the lives of others, or remind them of their original purpose for choosing a particular job path.

Assessing the Ethics Training Workshops

Workshop attendees and the facilitator should assess the training session at its conclusion. The following is a checklist of some items that could be included on a training effectiveness checklist:[21]

- Were specific real-life situations addressed?
- Were questions raised by participants?
- Were participants shown how to correct ethical problems?
- Were the situations raised linked back to the Code of Ethics, Code of Conduct, or organizational strategy?
- Did the trainer serve as a coach and facilitator, rather than a lecturer?

Summary

Many organizations recognize the need to conduct ethics training for employees at all levels of the organization. Web-based ethics training is appealing because of its homogeneity and low costs. However, the best ethics training involves dialogue regarding real-life situations experienced at work.

This chapter recommended 10 different ethics training workshops. The workshops should be staggered over time. Continually improve ethical performance by praising the good, developing and implementing strategies to overcome the weaknesses, and assessing the results.

Notes

1. Sean Valentine and Gary Fleischman, "Ethics Training and Businesspersons' Perceptions of Organizational Ethics," *Journal of Business Ethics*, 52, no. 4 (2004): 381–390.

2. David Salierno, "Ethics Survey Offers Mixed Messages," *Internal Auditor*, 61, no. 3 (2004): 23–24; www.globalcompliance.com/pdf/BusinessEthicsandComplianceSurvey.pdf, accessed 9/9/08.

3. Jonathan West and Evan M. Berman, "Ethics Training in U.S. Cities," *Public Integrity*, 6, no. 3 (2004): 189–206.

4. Jane B. Romal and Arlene M. Hibschweiler, "Improving Professional Ethics," *CPA Journal*, 74, no. 6 (2004): 58–63.

5. Barry Spizer, "Log On for Free Ethics Course," *Commercial Investment Real Estate Journal*, 22, no. 3 (2004): 4; the course is available online at www.ccim.com/ethicscourse/htm.

6. www.aicpa.org/Magazines+and+Newsletters/Newsletters/The+CPA+Letter/Disciplinary+Actions/default.htm, accessed 9/10/08.

7. Jean Thilmany, "Supporting Ethical Employees," *HRMagazine*, 52, no. 9 (2007): 105–112.

8. Ronald E. Berenbein, *Universal Conduct—An Ethics and Compliance Benchmarking Survey*, The Conference Board Report 1393-06-RR, 2006.

9. Samuel Greengard, "Golden Values at Coors," *Workforce Management*, March 2005: 52-53.

10. Joseph Weber, "The New Ethics Enforcers," *Business Week*, February 13, 2006: 76-77.

11. www.jeopardy.com/interstitial.php, accessed 9/10/08.

12. www.millionairetv.com/, accessed 9/10/08.

13. www.dod.mil/dodgc/defense_ethics/dod_oge/Encyclopedia_of_Ethical_Failures_2007_Full_Version.doc, accessed 9/10/08.

14. Steven R. Barth, *Corporate Ethics* (Boston, MA: Aspatore Books, 2003): 102–119.

15. Julian B. Rotter, "Some Problems and Misconceptions Related to the Construct of Internal versus External Control of Reinforcement," *Journal of Consulting and Clinical Psychology*, 43, 1 (1975): 56–67.

16. http://www.ballarat.edu.au/ard/bssh/psych/rot.htm, accessed 9/10/08.

17. Linda Klebe Trevino and Stuart A. Youngblood, "Bad Apples in Bad Barrels: A Causal Analysis of Ethical Decision-Making Behavior," *Journal of Applied Psychology*, 75, no. 4 (1990): 378–385.

18. Richard Christie and Florence I. Geis, *Studies in Machiavellianism* (New York: Academic Press, 1970).

19. National Specialty Insurance (NSI), a division of West Bend Mutual Insurance Company.

20. Matthew Fox, *The Reinvention of Work* (San Francisco: Harper-Collins, 1995).

21. Walter O. Baggett, "7 Criteria for Ethics Assessments," *Internal Auditor*, 64, 1 (2007): 65–69.

CHAPTER 7

Respecting Employee Diversity

- Describe five competitive advantages of diversity
- Implement a diversity initiative
- Adopt best operational practices for managing diversity
- Conduct a variety of diversity workshops
- Manage different communication styles

The population of the United States continues to diversify, as does the employee and customer base of organizations.

For more than two centuries, the American workforce was dominated by European-American males. This is no longer the situation. In 2004, European-American men made up only 36% of the entire workforce; European-American women composed one-third, followed by Latino-Americans (14%), African-Americans (12%), and Asian-Americans (4%).[1]

The purchasing power of minorities continues to escalate as well. In 2007, the combined buying power of African-Americans, Asian-Americans, and Native Americans was $1.4 trillion, triple that from two decades earlier.[2] Latino-American disposable income accounts for 10% of all spending.

This chapter describes the many competitive advantages of appropriately managing diversity. A Seven-step process for implementing a diversity initiative is offered, along with best practices for managing diversity. Instructions are provided for conducting a series of diversity exercises that increase social group self-awareness, explore specific issues, and help employees manage different communication styles.

Competitive Advantages of Diversity Management

Every employee should feel comfortable at work, and every customer and supplier should feel comfortable doing business with any organization. But that is not always the case.

Like attracts like, and individuals relate best with people similar to themselves. Problems arise when dissimilar people are treated as inferior or excluded. Customers and employees who differ from others according to some prominent characteristic—race, gender, ethnicity, age, or religion—often report not being respected by the dominant social group. This typically damages employee morale, productivity, customer relations, revenue, and profits, and can result in litigation.

The avoidance of lawsuits and increased government regulation are fear-based incentives for respecting diversity. Five positive bottom-line reasons why respecting diversity creates a competitive advantage for organizations are:

1. *To attract and retain diverse customers:* Customers tend to feel more comfortable doing business with people who respect them. Customers from diverse social groups who feel unwelcomed by insensitive sales people from a different social group will take their business elsewhere.

2. *To attract and retain diverse employees:* As an organization's reputation for appropriately managing diversity issues increases, so does the diversity of the organization's job applicant pool.

3. *To achieve cost reductions:* Cost reductions associated with diversity management include fewer employee grievances, absences, turnover, and litigation. Responding to claims that an employee is being discriminated against requires time and resources to resolve.

4. *To enhance decision making, problem solving, and creativity:* Different cultural groups perceive the world in different ways, due to different life experiences, enhancing organizational decision making, problem solving, and creativity. A multicultural workforce is likely to make more informed decisions regarding their own cultural groups, and examine an issue from multiple perspectives.

5. *To increase stakeholder goodwill:* Organizations that are diversity leaders earn goodwill from the media, government, socially conscious consumers, and job candidates wanting to contribute to a broad social mission. This translates into free advertising from the media and consumers, and high-profile government and industry task forces.

Four Layers of Diversity

Understanding the nature of diversity must precede developing the skills necessary to appropriately manage diversity. Every person is diverse, and we tend to take our own diversity for granted.

Diversity can be conceptualized on four unique layers: internal personality dimension, unchanging external dimension, evolving external dimension, and organizational dimension. Each layer of diversity adds complexity to who we are and how others perceive us.

Internal Personality Dimensions

Employees can be categorized according to their internal personality, which is the inner core of human existence. The Myers-Briggs Type Indicator (MBTI), probably the most popular personality assessment tool,[3] is based on four dimensions, each with a paired continuum—introvert versus extrovert, sensing versus intuition, thinking versus feeling, and perceiving versus judging. As with zodiac signs, none of the 16 MBTI profiles are better than another. Each MBTI profile has different strengths and weaknesses in terms of leadership style, working with others, and conflict resolution.

Unchanging External Dimensions

Employees can be categorized according to external characteristics as well as internal ones. External human characteristics that are permanent and beyond a person's control include race, ethnicity, gender, sexual orientation, and birth generation. A person who is born a caucasian, Italian-American, male, heterosexual, baby boomer remains so throughout life.

Evolving External Dimensions

Employees can be categorized according to evolving external characteristics as well as unchanging ones. External characteristics that evolve over time include age, height, weight, religion, education, physical ability, marital status, income level, and geographic location. At one point in life an employee is categorized as a young person, and treated accordingly, and later in life the same person is categorized as an older person, and treated accordingly.

Organizational Dimensions

Employees can also be categorized according to their organizational status. These defining characteristics—which can be either unchanging or evolving—include hierarchical status, work content, department, and seniority. Some employees are classified as nonmanagement, others as management. The "in group" at Enron consisted of Gas Bank Division employees with degrees in economics or finance (see *In the Real World: Checks and Balances—1997*). Members of other diverse populations were expected to be subservient to them.

IN THE REAL WORLD

Checks and Balances—1997

Michael Kopper agreed to Andy Fastow's plan for funding the RADR SPE, and everyone involved profited.

(Continued)

IN THE REAL WORLD (CONTINUED)

In early 1997, David Duncan, a relatively young rising star and Arthur Andersen partner at age 38, became Andersen's lead auditor on the Enron account. He would be reviewing the work of his former boss at Andersen, Rick Causey, now Enron's chief accounting officer (CAO). Duncan was a strong client advocate, someone who helped clients achieve desired accounting objectives. His annual bonus and advancement within Andersen depended on increasing client fees by 20%. Enron was Duncan's only customer. Critically questioning Enron's accounting transactions and financial arrangements could mean career suicide, something Fastow and Skilling pointed out to Duncan and his subordinates.

Fastow's creative SPE schemes saved Enron's fourth-quarter 1997 financial performance. Cash flow went from a negative $588 million at the end of September to a positive $501 million at the end of December, a $1 billion change for a company not dependent on Christmas sales.

Carl Bass, a senior Andersen accountant on Duncan's audit team, objected to Enron's aggressive accounting methods. Bass, having worked on the Enron account for two years, had developed a low regard for both Fastow and Causey. Bass concluded that Enron was inappropriately booking income and that Duncan should not sign off on the 1997 fourth quarter audited statements until the company applied more rigorous accounting methods. This action would be interpreted negatively by Wall Street investors.

Fastow threatened to change accounting firms if Duncan did not sign the audited statements. Duncan, as the lead engagement partner, has the final say in the matter.

DECISION CHOICE. If you were the lead external auditor engagement partner on the Enron account, would you:

> ❶ Risk losing the Enron account, which is the basis for your career path within Andersen, by demanding that Fastow and Causey follow more rigorous accounting methods?
>
> ❷ Risk your professional license by allowing Fastow and Causey to use aggressive accounting methods?
>
> Why?

Implementing a Diversity Initiative

Creating an organizational culture that respects diversity requires planning and effort. This would only "naturally" happen if all employees were raised by highly enlightened parents in highly diverse neighborhoods.

The following is a 10-step process for implementing successful diversity initiatives based on a traditional organizational change model.[4]

1. *Present a business case for the diversity initiative:* Determine which of the five competitive advantages of diversity discussed earlier is most important for achieving superior organizational performance. Use this reason as the key motivator for undertaking the diversity initiative. Support the rationale with demographic trends, competitive analysis, and adoption of best practices in the industry.

2. *Create a shared vision statement:* People implementing the diversity initiative must be committed to achieving the desired results. Achieve commitment by involving them in the crafting of a vision statement emphasizing fair treatment of all stake-

holders. Clearly link the diversity vision to the competitive advantage.

3. *Respectfully build from the past:* The diversity initiative is one step along the continuous improvement path, though it could be a giant one at that. Praise previous successes and use past success as the foundation for new initiatives.

4. *Create a sense of urgency:* The time for change is now, ahead of the competition, not later, after the competition has already staked its claim in the diverse markets and talent pools.

5. *Empower a change agent:* All organizational changes require a point person ultimately accountable for achieving the desired results. Give a particular "go-to" person authority to manage the change process.

6. *Gather political support:* Success depends on all work units supporting the diversity initiative. Educate all formal and informal leaders about the importance of the change initiative. Establish a diversity committee composed of key supporting people to oversee the initiative.

7. *Craft an implementation plan:* Gather input from those directly affected by the changes. Anticipate, and overcome, obstacles by inviting representatives from the affected organizational units and diversity groups to comment on the implementation plan. Link action plan strategies to reasonable long-term and short-term goals.

8. *Develop enabling processes:* Train key participants to manage the change process. Establish multiple communication channels for input and feedback on the quality and quantity of changes being

made. Share feedback and results with key constituents. Revise the plan as needed.

9. *Evaluate the progress:* Gather relevant historical data to benchmark and measure progress toward achieving the stated goals and objectives. Recognize all positive changes. In the spirit of continuous improvement, explore unmet goals with key constituents.

10. *Reinforce the change:* Link the accomplishment of diversity objectives to performance evaluations and compensation. Spotlight diversity champions and share their best practices. Rewards and visibility reinforce credibility.

Best Operational Practices for Managing Diversity

In 1998, the Equal Employment Opportunity Commission Task Force published examples of the "best" diversity policies, programs, and practices in the private sector.[5] Integrate these best practices in diversity management throughout organizational operations to ensure long-term continuous success.

- *Diversity office/committee/officer:* Assign organizational responsibility for diversity to a diversity office, committee, or officer.

- *Recruiting and hiring:* Develop a list of highly qualified diverse job candidates that employees know, and personally invite them to apply. Sources include previous business dealings, professional associations, civic organizations, school and volunteer activities, minority job fairs and publications, and internship programs for colleges and high schools with high minority populations.

- *Personnel policies:* Rather than a one-size-fits-all approach, provide flexible personnel policies reflecting the needs of diverse populations Areas for flexibility include the use of personal days, cafeteria-style benefits plans, and work schedules.

- *Dispute resolution mechanisms:* Be receptive to diversity-related grievances. Presume everyone innocent until proven otherwise. The most efficient dispute resolution system is a direct dialogue between both parties. If unsuccessful, have a supervisor or Diversity Officer serve as mediator. If unsuccessful, have a Peer Review Panel arbitrate a binding resolution.

- *Retention and promotions:* Diversity retention techniques that lead to promotions include job training and rotation, challenging assignments, holistic performance appraisals, career counseling, mentoring, focus group feedback, and promotion from within.

- *Performance appraisals:* Link bonuses to achieving diversity goals. Include a performance appraisal scale measuring behaviors that demonstrate respect for diverse coworkers and customers.

- *Termination and downsizing:* The two best criteria for determining layoffs are job requirements and past performance. When organizations use a seniority criterion, newly hired diverse employees are the first to be terminated, undoing years of concerted effort to diversify the workforce. Conduct an adverse impact analysis to determine if the list of employees to be laid off adversely affects the percentage of women, racial, and ethnic minorities employed by the organization.

TIPS AND TECHNIQUES

Diversity Training Goals

It takes time and effort to develop a safe and supportive work environment that respects diverse people. All employees need to be trained to appropriately interact with diverse populations of customers and coworkers.

Two important goals of diversity training goals are to:

❶ Eliminate values, stereotypes, and managerial practices that inhibit the personal and professional development of diverse employees.

❷ Allow diverse employees to contribute their best efforts for achieving superior organizational performance.

Diversity Training Problems and Solutions

Helping employees overcome their biases toward diverse people can be a difficult task. Exhibit 7.1 summarizes seven diversity training problems and their recommended solutions. The "dominant group" refers to the diverse characteristic that is held in common by a large number of employees, such as a particular gender, race, or ethnic group. The "subordinate group" refers to the diversity characteristic held by a small minority of organizational members.

Carefully frame diversity training workshops so that they will be well-received by all employees. Begin the diversity training workshop by discussing the five competitive advantages of diversity presented earlier. The purpose of diversity training is to improve organizational performance and profitability.

EXHIBIT 7.1

Diversity Training Problems and Solutions

Problem	Solution
The trainer lacks credibility with either the dominant group or the subordinated group.	Use workshop co-leaders, one from the dominant group and one from the subordinated group. They can model positive behaviors through their interactions managing the workshop.
The organization's diversity problems are portrayed too negatively.	Begin the workshop by recognizing the efforts of diversity champions so that others may rally around them. Then discuss organizational shortcomings.
Employees from the dominant group are portrayed too negatively.	Begin the workshop by recognizing how particular members of the dominant group have succeeded in managing diversity. Then challenge everyone to do even more.
Training is limited to the dominant group (usually European-American male prejudices).	Prejudices are not unique to any one particular demographic group. Explore everyone's prejudices, those of both the dominant group and the diverse groups.
Training exercises are not relevant.	Diversity training must improve work-related interactions between diverse people. Discuss real workplace situations.
Training emphasizes employee differences to the exclusion of common ground.	Despite our differences, diverse groups of people share many things in common with other diverse groups. Highlight these commonalities.

Training emphasizes knowledge and attitudes to the exclusion of behaviors.	Diversity training must eventually lead to behavioral changes at work. Clearly articulate and discuss specific acceptable and unacceptable behaviors. Practice rules of civil behavior.

Next, discuss some national and industry examples of diversity problems and their associated costs, such as Equal Employment Opportunity Commission cases filed and financial penalties assessed (see Exhibit 1.2 in Chapter 1). Employees need to understand that discrimination is a national and industry-wide problem; it is not unique to any particular organization.

Then educate employees about the best operational practices presented earlier in this chapter, so they can see what leading-edge organizations are doing to manage diversity.

Praise previous diversity efforts and change agents, and acknowledge the need for continuous improvement. Foster greater personal awareness of diversity issues, and develop action plans that improve diversity management.

Diversity Discussion Guidelines

Many employees are not comfortable discussing diversity issues. Some employees might respond to diversity issues in a manner that offends coworkers. Develop a list of appropriate discussion guidelines prior to delving into diversity issues on a more personal or organizational level.

Initial employee tension and resistance can be defused by a warm-up activity. A useful exercise is for the group to agree on discussion guidelines. Have attendees review the organization's existing discussion guidelines and make modifications as needed. If the organization lacks discussion guidelines, have participants independently develop a set of discussion guidelines, share them with the broader group, and reach consensus. These guidelines typically include being open and honest, participating fully at your own comfort level, listening respectfully, and maintaining confidentiality.

Diversity Training Exercises

The following sections highlight exercises for diversity workshops that are informative, relevant, and useful.

The first three diversity exercises foster self-awareness: Who Are You, Dominant Group and Subordinated Group Awareness, and White Privilege. The next two diversity exercises explore what it was like being prejudged, and how everyone is unique, yet shares things in common with others. The sixth diversity exercise focuses on generating discussion about sexual harassment. The last diversity exercise highlights a factor that is easily overlooked, yet can be the most damaging if not managed appropriately—differences in communication styles.

"Who Are You?" Exercise

No two people are alike. The "Who Are You?" exercise helps workshop participants understand their diverse uniqueness. Employees describe themselves according to the four layers of diversity, then discuss how these factors impact their attitudes and behaviors at work.

EXHIBIT 7.2

Who Are You?

Describe yourself using the four layers of diversity and discuss how these dimensions impact who you are.

- Describe your internal personality dimensions (i.e., Myers-Briggs Type Indicators).

- Describe your unchanging external dimensions (i.e., race, ethnicity, gender, sexual orientation, and birth generation).

- Describe your evolving external dimensions (i.e., age, height, weight, religion, education, physical ability, marital status, income level, and geographic location).

- Describe your organizational dimensions (i.e., hierarchical status, work content, department, and seniority).

- Which of these dimensions most strongly define who you are? How?

- Which of these dimensions impact how others treat you at work? How?

Dominant Group and Subordinated Group Awareness Exercise

Members of the dominant group tend to possess more power and influence over decisions and the shaping of organizational culture than subordinated group members. For instance, if all managers are European–American males (the dominant group), then European–American males have special status and their values shape organizational culture. This impact is much more obvious to subordinated group members than it is to dominant group members, who tend to take their special status for granted.

Exhibit 7.3 describes how the dominant and subordinated groups differ relative to several key workplace issues.

Have workshop attendees define their group membership as either the dominant group or subordinated group, and then examine how membership in this group impacts workplace performance.

EXHIBIT 7.3

Dominant/Subordinated Group Dynamics

Category	Dominant/Majority Group	Subordinated/Minority Group
Power	Has access to power	Needs access to power
Rules	Makes the rules	Adapts to the rules
Resources	Controls resources	Needs access to resources
Culture	Defines the culture	Struggles to fit in
Truth	Defines the truth	Has their truths and experience questioned and often invalidated
Normal	Seen as normal	Seen as inferior or as an exception to their group
Capable	Assumed to be capable (qualified)	Often assumed to be deficient (not qualified)
Benefit of Doubt	Given the benefit of doubt	Has to earn the benefit of doubt (has to "prove" they are qualified)
Awareness of Group Membership	Unaware of group membership	Very aware of group membership

Sense of Worth	Sees their group as the "best"	Internalized dominant group's beliefs reflected in lack of self worth, low self-esteem, or self-confidence
Behavior	Encourages subordinated group members to assimilate	Adapts; develops behaviors pleasing or accepting to dominant group members and cannot "show-up" too authentic or genuine
Treatment	Less aware of differential treatment	Very aware of differential treatment
Discrimination	Sees incidents of discrimination as individual actions that have little to do with group membership	Sees patterns of group level behavior based on repetitive nature

© 2008 Elsie Y. Cross Associates, Inc., www.eyca.com

White Privilege Exercise

Members of the dominant group are often unaware of the special status they have over subordinated groups. The White Privilege experiential exercise emphasizes many subtle aspects of white privilege in American society.[6]

Workshop participants line up with their backs to a wall, and up to 50 statements are sequentially read out loud. After each statement, participants who answer affirmatively take one step forward. Typically, after the last statement, European–American males are several steps ahead of the other social groups. Participants then turn around, face each other, and express their thoughts and feelings about the exercise.

Sample statements include:

1. I can turn on the television or open to the front page of the newspaper and see people of my race or gender widely represented in a positive manner.

2. I can do well in a challenging situation without being called a credit to my race or gender.

3. I can be pretty sure that if I ask to talk to the "person in charge," I will be facing a person of my race or gender.

Experiences being prejudged exercise

Every individual has been prejudged because of some notable characteristic—age, profession, geography, race, gender, religion, and so on. Exhibit 7.4 provides some prompt questions for workshop participants to answer on their own and then discuss in small groups.[7]

EXHIBIT 7.4

Experiences Being Prejudged Exercise

1. Describe how you have been stereotyped in a positive way. When did the incident occur? Where did the incident occur? Who said what to whom?

2. Describe how you have been stereotyped in a negative way. When did the incident occur? Where did the incident occur? Who said what to whom?

---

3. What were your reactions when the negative incident occurred? How did you feel? What did you think? What did you do?

4. What were the overall consequences of the negative incident? How did the incident affect you in the future? Did it change your expectations of yourself? Did it change your expectations of others?

Individual Uniqueness and Commonalities Exercise

People want to be treated as individuals, rather than as representatives of a social group. The exercise in Exhibit 7.5 helps employees understand how each of them is unique, and also how each of them shares some common traits with other members of the group.[8]

EXHIBIT 7.5

Individual Uniqueness and Commonalities Exercise

Step 1: Write down five things that make you unique within your group. For example: I was a vice president of my university student government, I had season tickets to New York Giants football games, I played center field on my baseball team and struck out a lot, I was a missionary, I came in second place for an 880-yard run in grade school (though there were only two other people running in the race).

1.
2.
3.
4.
5.

Step 2: Share your items with your group members and circle those that are still unique.

Step 3: Have an informal discussion with your group members and find five things that you have in common with other members of your group.

1.
2.
3.
4.
5.

Sexual Harassment Exercise

The Equal Employment Opportunity Commission differentiates between two types of sexual harassment—quid pro quo and hostile environment.[9]

Quid pro quo sexual harassment occurs when conditions of employment or employment decisions are dependent on unwelcome sexual advances, requests for sexual favors, or other verbal or physical conduct of a sexual nature.

A "hostile environment" occurs when any of these three conditions interferes with an individual's work performance. In determining the degree of hostility, judges typically consider the frequency and severity of the conduct, and whether it is an offensive utterance or physically threatening.

An organization can be liable for an employee sexually harassing a coworker if the employer either knows, or should have known, of the harassment and failed to take reasonable corrective action.

In small groups, discuss whether the four scenarios that follow constitute sexual harassment. Do they create a "hostile environment" at work? Other scenarios can be developed by employees who believe that they have been sexually harassed, or have been accused of sexual harassment.

Scenario One: Jess is Kim's administrative assistant. Every morning Kim makes flattering comments about Jess' appearance.

Scenario Two: Jess is Kim's administrative assistant. Kim invites Jess out for drinks to a singles bar after work. Jess claims not to be available. One week later Kim invites Jess out for drinks after work again.

Scenario Three: Jess is Kim's administrative assistant. Kim is an affectionate person and gently touches the arms of both male and female workers while engaged in conversation. Kim gently touches Jess' arms three or four times a day.

Scenario Four: Jess is Kim's administrative assistant. Kim receives several unsolicited junk e-mails a day, including those about improving sexual performance. One of these unsolicited sexual performance e-mails is quite humorous, and Kim forwards the e-mail to Jess.

Communication Style Exercise

Communication style is an often overlooked aspect of employee diversity. People tend to express themselves in a way that feels natural to them and assume that others like to communicate in the same manner. But this disrespects the uniqueness of the person receiving the information, results in misunderstandings, and negatively impacts employee performance.

Treating others with respect means understanding how other people prefer to communicate. This can be very difficult and strenuous, because the initiator of the communication must convey information in a way that the other person prefers to receive information, rather than in the way that comes natural to the communication initiator.

For instance, people who get right to the point typically assume that the person they are communicating with wants to get right to the point. They also prefer that others communicating with them get right to the point. If the other person does not, the other person is considered distracted or wasting time.

Some people, however, first ask about the other person's family situation instead of getting right to the point. People who first make a personal connection assume that the person they are communicating with wants to first make a personal connection. They also prefer that others communicating with them make a personal connection. If the other person does not, the other person is considered rude or uncaring.

Rhonda Hilyer has developed a very useful tool of four communication styles, each symbolized by a different color.[10] Individuals can exhibit all four styles to some extent, but most likely one or two styles dominate. The four communication styles are summarized in Exhibit 7.6.

EXHIBIT 7.6

Communication Styles

Brown

- Direct, brief, and decisive
- Focuses on tasks and results
- Assertive
- Desires "yes/no" or "black/white" answers
- Doesn't want a lot of detail
- Stays on point
- Impatient if things move too slowly

Green

- Logical, sequential, and focused on details
- Desires historical data
- Literal and factual
- Appears reserved and avoids emotions
- Needs time to process information
- A planner, precise and organized

Blue

- Concerned with how others feel and will be affected
- Supportive and agreeable
- Includes others in the decision-making process
- Likes to chat and form a personal connection before getting on task
- Good listener

Red

- Flamboyant, dramatic, and energetic
- Fast-paced
- Frequently tells jokes or stories
- Tends to over-generalize for effect
- Likes humor and creative ideas
- Spontaneous, innovative, and enthusiastic

Have workshop participants identify which of the four colors best represents:

- Their own communication style
- Their boss's communication style
- Their subordinate's communication style
- A peer's communication style
- The communication style of the person they struggle with the most at work

Next, help employees understand how coworkers perceive their communication style. For instance, request that all participants with a brown communication style stand in front of the workshop. Then ask coworkers who struggle with browns to express what they appreciate about the brown style and how they are sometimes frustrated or confused by the brown style. This process helps browns understand how others react to their communication style. In addition, coworkers realize that their struggles with the brown might be a result of the communication style differences rather than with the person.

Then do the same with the other three communication styles.

If an employee wants to influence a coworker, the employee should practice conveying information using the coworker's communication style. Doing so results in a more harmonious communication experience and successful conveyance of information.

- If the employee wants to influence a brown, practice communicating in a direct manner with a brown.

- If the employee wants to influence a blue, practice discussing a blue's life situation prior to asking the blue to do something.

- If the employee wants to influence a green, practice providing a green with a great deal of detail relevant to the issue being discussed.

- If the person wants to influence a red, practice communicating with a red in a fun and expressive manner.

Summary

Ethical organizations respect diverse employees and customers, and doing so creates many competitive advantages over other organizations. This chapter summarized how to implement a diversity initiative and best operational practices for managing diversity. Common diversity training problems were highlighted and addressed. A wide variety of diversity workshop exercises were reviewed, ranging from self-awareness to enhancing organizational performance by understanding different communication styles. All of these diversity activities directly impact an organization's financial performance.

Notes

1. Norma Carr-Ruffino, *Managing Diversity: People Skills for a Multicultural Workplace*, 7th edition (Boston, MA: Pearson Custom Publishing, 2006): 4.

2. Kathryn A. Canas and Harris Sondak, *Opportunities and Challenges of Workplace Diversity* (Upper Saddle River, NJ: Pearson Prentice Hall, 2008): 6.

3. www.myersbriggs.org, accessed 9/10/08.

4. Rosabeth Kanter, Barry Stein, and Todd Jick (eds.), *The Challenge of Organizational Change* (New York: Free Press, 1992).

5. Equal Employment Opportunity Commission (EEOC), *Best Practices of Private Sector Employers* (Washington, D.C.: Equal Employment Opportunity Commission, 1998); available at www.eeoc.gov/abouteeoc/task_reports/practice.html, accessed 9/11/08.

6. Peggy McIntosh, "White Privilege and Male Privilege: A Personal Account of Coming To See Correspondences through Work in Women's Studies," *Peace and Freedom*, July/August 1989.

7. Anne McKee and Susan Schor, "Confronting Prejudice and Stereotypes: A Teaching Model," *Journal of Management Education*, 18, 4 (1994): 447–467.

8. Ibid.

9. www.hr-guide.com/data/G703.htm, accessed 9/11/08.

10. Rhonda Hilyer, *Success Signals*, 7th edition (Seattle, Washington: Agreement Dynamics, 2006). For more information, contact Agreement Dynamics at: 1-800-97-AGREE or HQ@agreementdynamics.com.

PART 3

Daily Internal Operations

CHAPTER 8

Ethics Reporting Systems

After reading this chapter, you will be able to:

- Administer an internal reporting system for ethical issues
- Create an ethics & compliance officer (ECO) position
- Establish an ombudsman position
- Manage an assist line to receive employee complaints by telephone or Internet
- Describe the negative outcomes whistleblowing has on both the whistleblower and the organization

Organizations must open avenues of communication among all employees to discuss ethical issues as they arise. An employee uncomfortable sharing such information with his or her direct manager needs other outlets.

This chapter explores three internal communication mechanisms for obtaining information about unethical behavior: an ethics &

compliance officer (ECO), an ombudsman, and an assist line. A failure in these internal communication systems can result in external whistleblowing, which is damaging for both the organization and the whistleblower.

Undesirable Employee Reactions to Ethical Issues

Many employees are hesitant to reveal ethical problems to their supervisor or executives. As a result, employees see unethical conduct, but often don't do anything about it. According to the Ethics Resource Center's 2005 National Business Ethics Survey, this is because:[1]

- 59% believe no corrective action will be taken
- 46% fear retaliation
- 39% fear no anonymity
- 24% assumed someone else would report it
- 18% did not know who to contact

Organizations must establish communication systems for receiving this information. Someone in the organization must be held accountable for overseeing that the ethical problems are addressed, the information is held in confidentiality, and the employee providing the information is protected from retaliation.

If an appropriate ethics reporting system is not available, employees are left with two options damaging to the organization. The employee can either remain quiet as the situation worsens or damage the organization's reputation by blowing the whistle to a public authority.

Ethics & Compliance Officer (ECO)

The Federal Sentencing Guidelines (see Chapter 2) provide a judicial incentive for assigning a high-level employee the responsibility of managing ethical performance. Giving ethics high visibility demonstrates a good faith effort to enhance ethics within the organization, which may reduce judicial penalties.

A growing number of organizations assign this responsibility to an ECO. The position enables sensitive information to be shared without being diluted or stymied by the chain of command. There are more than 4,000 ECOs nationwide. The number will continue to grow, because new laws, such as the Sarbanes-Oxley Act, require greater institutional support for monitoring ethical behavior.[2]

The Ethics & Compliance Officer Association (ECOA), a professional organization for managers of ethics, compliance, and business conduct programs, has more than 1,200 members from a wide range of industries.

Some organizations create a separate ECO position focused solely on enhancing ethical performance.[3] Many organizations, however, add the title and job responsibilities to an existing position, such as legal counsel, ombudsman, regulatory compliance manager, internal auditor, or human resources manager.

Organizations also differ according to the nature and scope of ECO activities. Some organizations are highly centralized: One person or office determines ethics activities and standards for the entire organization. Other organizations are highly decentralized. The ECO provides oversight and the different locations or markets create their own ethics activities and standards, allowing for greater flexibility.

ECO Duties and Skills

What does an ECO do? ECO duties and responsibilities include:[4]

- Manage internal reporting systems
- Assess areas for ethical risks
- Offer guidance
- Monitor the organization's adherence to its Code of Ethics and Code of Conduct
- Oversee the ethics communication strategy
- Develop and interpret ethics policies
- Oversee the ethics training program
- Receive information about potential wrongdoings
- Collect and analyze relevant data
- Ensure that decisions are made and enforced
- Inform employees about outcomes

TIPS AND TECHNIQUES

Ethics & Compliance Officer (ECO) Attributes

An ECO receives very sensitive information about organizational behaviors that must be managed in a delicate manner.

An ECO should be someone who has:[5]

- Insider status and is well-networked with business unit managers
- A high position that exemplifies authority
- The trust and respect of organizational executives
- Independence from senior staff and freedom from internal political pressure
- Operational experience
- Knowledge of organizational issues and activities
- Access to internal information as needed
- Knowledge of ethical theories
- Counseling and communication skills
- Problem-solving skills

Every employee contact is essential because it only takes one unethical activity to severely damage an organization's operations.

ECOs respond to a wide range of practical questions, such as gift-giving with suppliers and customers, or personal use of organizational property. Employees often need clarity on these types of questions because of situational nuances. Many organizations, for instance, have an ethics policy stating that employees should not receive substantial gifts from vendors. But how much money is a substantial amount, and what if the gift is the result of winning a raffle at an industry conference?

The need to consider situational nuances is a major advantage of employing an ECO. The connection is personal, and the ECO can ask probing questions that explore extenuating circumstances. *In the Real World: Code of Ethics Exemption Request—June 1999* provides an extenuating circumstance presented to Enron's Board of Directors regarding the application of the company's Code of Ethics.

IN THE REAL WORLD

Code of Ethics Exemption Request—June 1999

David Duncan, the lead Arthur Andersen auditor on the Enron account, ignored his colleague's concerns and supported Andy Fastow's and CAO Rick Causey's aggressive interpretation of accounting rules. As a result, Enron nearly doubled its annual profits for 1997, from $54 million to $105 million.

Beginning in 1999, with Wall Street experiencing a bull market and Enron's stock continually rising, Lay and Skilling expanded into new trading markets, including minerals, by acquiring an average of two companies a month. Under Skilling's direction, Enron evolved from a natural gas pipeline company to a trading company, with traders accounting for a third of its 15,000 employees.

Ken Lay and Jeff Skilling were now on center stage in a global economy, providing for people's heating, electricity, and water needs across the Earth. Revenue shot up accordingly, from $13.3 billion in 1996 to $31 billion in 1998.

Skilling promoted Fastow to CFO of Enron. Fastow structured an SPE named LJM1 to support a network of financially troubled SPEs doing business with, or on behalf of, Enron. If this network of SPEs failed, Enron would experience tremendous financial strain.

Fastow told Skilling that outsiders would invest in the risky LJM1 only if Fastow was its managing partner. Enron's Code of Ethics prohibited executives from participating in a company doing business with Enron, so Fastow would need to be exempted from this policy. Skilling approved the exemption and Lay did likewise. The final step in the exemption approval process required approval by Enron's Board of Directors.

Lay, Skilling, and Duncan attended the June 28, 1999 Board of Directors meeting. Fastow explained why it was essential for him to serve as a managing partner of LJM1 and, thus, exempted from the relevant Code of Ethics policy. To safeguard against any potential conflict of interest, every deal between Enron and LJM1 would be presented to the Board of Directors for final approval. As an additional safeguard, LJM1's financial statements would be audited by the public accounting firm KPMG, rather than Arthur Andersen, so two accounting firms would be reviewing the fairness of all LJM1 transactions with Enron.

DECISION CHOICE. If you were on Enron's Board of Directors would you:

❶ Exempt Fastow from Enron's Code of Ethics, given the established accounting safeguards?

❷ Refuse to exempt Fastow and cause the financial failure of an entire set of SPEs heavily invested in by Enron?

Why?

Managing an Internal Reporting System

The ECO's primary duty is to manage the organization's internal reporting system. The process model in Exhibit 8.1 provides guidance on how to accomplish this.[6]

Ombudsman

Another channel for communicating information about potential ethical and legal violations is an organizational ombudsman. The

EXHIBIT 8.1

Internal Reporting System Process

Step	Activity
1.	Develop the ethics reporting policy in partnership with upper management to establish their buy-in.
2.	Communicate the ethics reporting policy to all employees through multiple media, such as the employee handbook, e-mail, the company intranet site, department meetings, and training sessions.
3.	Emphasize the importance of reporting concerns about unethical and illegal conduct. Management cannot act on what it does not know.
4.	Assure people that any form of retaliation against an employee who raises an ethical concern is prohibited.
5.	If appropriate, the employee should first attempt to resolve the issue by directly approaching the individual engaged in the questionable activity.
6.	If direct discussion or resolution is not possible, then the employee should confidentially meet with the ECO to discuss the issue.
7.	If the employee prefers not to reveal his or her identity, then the employee should anonymously submit the concern to the ECO through the organization's intranet reporting system or in a sealed box. Establish a means of communication if the issue becomes a high-priority item needing additional information from the employee.
8.	Following Step 6 or Step 7, assure the employee that his or her identity will not be revealed without consent.
9.	Interview the employee and discuss clarifying questions.
10.	Develop a plan for investigating the case in a manner that honors the employee's confidentiality or anonymity.
11.	Conduct the investigation in a fair and confidential manner.
12.	If the investigation reveals that the employee's allegations are accurate, take prompt action to correct the wrongdoing.

13. Inform the employee about the outcome of the investigation.
14. Establish an appeals process for employees dissatisfied with the outcome of the initial investigation. Provide an advocate, probably from the human resources department, to assist an employee who wishes to appeal an outcome.

ombudsman concept originated in government, and has spread to other types of organizations, such as corporations, hospitals, newspapers, universities, and nonprofits.

An ombudsman's job scope is typically much narrower than that of an ECO. An ombudsman guarantees the employee anonymity, investigates the employee's concern, mediates a fair settlement, and protects the employee from retaliation. By providing employees with an institutional voice, the ombudsman serves as a deterrent against managerial abuse of power and other unethical activities. The ombudsman is granted access to all employees, including board members, when investigating a complaint.

An ombudsman, similar to lawyers and accountants, is held legally accountable to a professional Code of Ethics. The International Ombudsman Association's Code of Ethics highlights four ethical principles and corresponding policies:[7]

1. *Independence.* The ombudsman is independent in structure, function, and appearance to the highest degree possible within the organization.
2. *Neutrality and impartiality.* The ombudsman remains unaligned and impartial, and does not engage in any situation which could create a conflict of interest.

3. *Confidentiality.* The ombudsman holds all communications in strict confidence, and does not disclose confidential communications unless given permission to do so. The only exception to this privilege of confidentiality is when there is an imminent risk of serious harm.

4. *Informality.* The ombudsman does not participate in any formal adjudicative or administrative procedure related to concerns brought to his/her attention.

Three Types of Ombudsman

Three distinct types of ombudsman are classical-ombudsman, mediator-ombudsman, and advocate-ombudsman.[8]

The classical-ombudsman is the most practical model for organizations to adopt. After discussing the issue with the employee, the ombudsman asks permission to contact key people, develops a plan for gathering information without revealing the identity of the complainant, investigates the claim outside the regular chain of command, reaches a conclusion, and then advocates for implementing the appropriate change.

A mediator-ombudsman maintains neutrality, proposes options to the disputing parties, and focuses on reaching an agreeable resolution. Implementing the solution becomes someone else's responsibility, which detracts from the effectiveness of the mediator-ombudsman model.

An advocate-ombudsman is more likely to be found in government than other types of organizations. The advocate-ombudsman pursues justice on behalf of the person submitting the complaint.

The primary problem with the advocate-ombudsman model is that an adversarial relationship is created between the ombudsman and managers involved in the situation.

Organizational Issues Addressed

Putnam Investments employs an ombudsman. Employees are encouraged to contact the ombudsman for any of the following issues:[9]

- A code of ethics violation
- Trading issues or violations
- Legal or compliance issues
- A situation that threatens employee safety
- Unfair treatment by a manager or coworker
- Unfair pay as defined in the Fair Labor Standards Act
- Unfair treatment on the basis of sex, race, color, ethnic group, age, sexual orientation, or other affiliation

Assist Lines

Assist lines, previously referred to as "ethics hotlines," have long been popular with organizations as a method of obtaining information about situations that may be unethical or illegal. Nearly all Fortune 500 companies provide toll-free assist lines for employees from all over the world to share their concerns.

Professional organizations also provide assist lines for members who prefer to confidentially address issues with someone not employed by his or her organization. The AICPA's Professional

Ethics Division offers members two types of confidential assist lines, one by telephone and the other by e-mail.[10]

Types of Inquiries

Many organizations now refer to this communication channel as an assist line rather than an ethics hotline for two reasons.

The phrase "ethics hotline" makes it seem as though the employee is snitching or squealing on someone, an impression that managers should avoid. In addition, "assist" more accurately describes most of the calls that are received. According to Sears, whose assist line receives 16,000 to 18,000 calls a year from its 300,000 employees, only a very small percentage of the calls report potential law violations.[11]

The largest group of assist line callers consists of employees asking for assistance to solve a human resources issue, such as how to respond to an unfavorable performance evaluation or lack of work breaks. These types of inquiries are not the original intention of an assist line. Nonetheless, organizations should welcome these types of comments in the spirit of continuous improvement and because employees are able to express their frustrations.

The second largest group of assist line callers consists of employees asking for ethics policy clarifications. This is a good sign, because employees are asking for clarification before the fact, rather than being reported for committing a violation after the fact.

Effective Assist Lines

Two major issues must be addressed to enhance the effectiveness of assist lines: confidentiality and false accusations.

Employees may doubt that the assist line is really confidential or anonymous. Honor confidentiality at all times. Word of any confidentiality breaches without the employee's permission will quickly spread and prevent other employees from using the system.

Employees may fear that the assist line will generate false accusations from someone seeking revenge for a bad performance appraisal or competing for an internal job opening. Clearly state that all assist line submissions must be offered in good faith and anyone who purposely submits a false accusation will be disciplined.

How an Assist Line Works

EthicsPoint, founded in 1999 by a group of certified fraud examiners, is used by many corporations, universities, nonprofits, and government agencies.[12] An employee anonymously contacts EthicsPoint by e-mail or telephone and receives a confidential case identification number. Employees who are comfortable with the system can provide their names, but this is not required.

The response system is scripted to gather as much information as possible from an anonymous employee. The information is categorized based on type of issue and operations area, and then anonymously routed to the appropriate manager at the employee's organization. The submission will not be routed to any person named in the inquiry.

For colleges and universities, the EthicsPoint system highlights four categories of wrongdoing:

1. *Unethical financial abuse, such as fraud.*
2. *Unethical personal conduct, such as discrimination.*

3. *Unethical treatment of college property, such as theft.*

4. *Unethical use of information technology, such as data privacy abuse.*

An "other" category is available for issues that do not fit any of these four options.

The organizational manager receiving the information responds to the EthicsPoint system using the case identification number. The manager can submit additional questions for the employee to anonymously answer, or clarify any misunderstandings about the organization's policy on the issue. The anonymous employee can trace the case's progress using the identification number.

These communications are filtered through EthicsPoint unless the employee who submitted the inquiry is willing to contact the manager directly.

Whistleblowing

This book is written for managers who are sincerely trying to create organizations of high integrity and superior performance. Many avenues for ethics communication have already been discussed: Annual Code of Ethics assessments, ethics training workshops, diversity training workshops, an ECO or ombudsman, and the installation of assist lines.

But sometimes a management or nonmanagement employee sincerely concerned about ethics works for an organization that refuses to take action against unethical or illegal activities. When this happens, the employee is faced with a major conflict of values—remain loyal to the organization or inform someone outside the organization who can take appropriate action.

Contacting someone outside the organization about misconduct inside the organization is referred to as whistleblowing. If nobody within the organization is willing to take action, then the employee can inform a regulator, lawyer, reporter, law enforcement official, or a watchdog group.

When to Blow the Whistle

Blowing the whistle on an employer can be very detrimental to both the organization and the whistleblower. Ideally, the following four conditions should be met before an employee informs an external authority:[13]

1. Serious harm is involved.
2. The whistleblower has already expressed his or her concerns to an immediate superior.
3. The whistleblower has exhausted other communication channels within the organization.
4. The whistleblower has convincing, documented evidence.

The False Claims Act

The federal government encourages whistleblowing. The False Claims Act was initially passed in 1863 during the Civil War to stop defense contractors from fraudulently selling the Union Army rifles, ammunition, and horses. Under a qui tam provision, citizens could sue the unscrupulous defense contractor on behalf of the government and be rewarded a percentage of the financial recovery.

The False Claims Act was strengthened in 1986 following a series of defense industry frauds against the federal government. An employee who independently sues his or her employer for fraud can now receive between 15–30% of the total recovery amount. If the government joins the lawsuit, the employee can receive up to 25% of the total recovery. The lawsuit must be filed within six years of the fraud being committed.

During the first 13 years of the 1986 law, whistleblowers received $340 million in qui tam payments.[14] Exhibit 8.2 lists the five highest settlements, all in the healthcare industry, as of January 2006.[15]

EXHIBIT 8.2

Top Five False Claims Acts Cases (as of January 25, 2006)

Settlement Amount	Company	Case
$900 million	Tenet Healthcare, 2006	Manipulating Medicare payments, kickbacks, and bill padding
$731.4 million	HCA (The Health Care Company), 2000	Billing for unnecessary lab tests that were not doctor ordered, upcoding medical problems to get higher reimbursements, and billing for non-reimbursable items
$631 million	HCA, 2003	Kickbacks to physicians and cost-reporting fraud
$567 million	Serono Group, 2005	Kickbacks to physicians for prescribing drug, kickbacks to pharmacies for recommending drug, and illegal marketing of drug

$559.4 million	Taketa-Abbott Pharmaceutical Products, 2001	Fraudulent drug pricing and marketing; gave doctors kickbacks by providing free samples with knowledge physicians would bill Medicare and Medicaid for them

Submission Considerations for False Claim Act Filings

According to the False Claims Act Legal Center, a potential whistleblower should consider the following prior to filing under the False Claims Act:[16]

- The whistleblower must have actual knowledge of the fraud, not just a suspicion, and the evidence cannot come from a publicly disclosed source, such as a newspaper or court record.

- The fraud cannot be a tax fraud; tax fraud is specifically exempt from prosecution under the False Claims Act.

- Federal money must be involved, or, in a state with a state False Claims Act, state money must be involved.

- Most lawyers work on a contingency fee basis, and will only pursue a case if the financial amount of the fraud is sizable, and the entity to be sued is able to pay back the stolen money and associated fines.

Whistleblower Protection Laws

Fear of retaliation is one of the primary reasons why employees do not blow the whistle on illegal activities.

According to the Sarbanes-Oxley Act of 2002, no publicly traded company, or subcontractor of that company, can discharge, demote, suspend, threaten, harass, or in any other manner discriminate against a whistleblower.[17] It also establishes criminal penalties for retaliation against whistleblowers of fines and imprisonment up to 10 years.

The number of whistleblower reports grew substantially after the legislation became law. In 2001, prior to the passage of the Sarbanes-Oxley Act, the SEC averaged 6,400 whistleblowing reports a month. Two years later, the monthly average escalated to 40,000.[18]

Negative Outcomes for Whistleblowers

The decision to blow the whistle on an employer should not be taken lightly. Blowing the whistle can have many negative impacts on an employee's life. Soon after blowing the whistle, many whistleblowers have experienced:[19]

1. Negative performance evaluations
2. Undesired job transfers
3. Demotions
4. Criticism or avoidance by coworkers
5. Physical, psychological, and family problems
6. Loss of job or forced retirement
7. Blacklisting impeding employment
8. Protracted legal battles waged at personal expense

Cynthia Cooper, for instance, was one of three whistleblowers awarded *Time* magazine's 2002 "Persons of the Year" for her courageous role in telling external authorities about WorldCom's massive accounting fraud. Her life, however, was a living nightmare just prior to, and after, blowing the whistle.[20] She experienced trouble sleeping during her secret internal audit investigation, knowing that the evidence meant some of her friends might go to jail. She was ostracized by her peers, who blamed her for job losses they experienced due to a massive corporate restructuring after the scandal became public, and suffered long bouts of depression, unable to do much beyond crying in bed all day.

Summary

Employees need multiple avenues to communicate information about potentially illegal or unethical conduct. Ethics & compliance officers, ombudsmen, and assist lines provide employees with an institutional mechanism for reporting unethical or illegal behaviors. These internal reporting systems must be carefully managed. Otherwise, the employee might externally blow the whistle, which can have significant negative ramifications for both the organization and the employee.

Notes

1. Ethics Resource Center, *How Employees View Ethics in Their Organizations 1994–2005* (Washington D.C.: Ethics Resource Center, 2005): 29.

2. www.theecoa.org, accessed 9/16/08.

3. Duffy A. Morf, Michael G. Schumacher, and Scott J. Vitell, "A Survey of Ethics Officers in Large Organizations," *Journal of Business Ethics, 20, no. 3 (1999): 265–271.*

4. Edward Petry, "Appointing an Ethics Officer," *Healthcare Executive*, 13, no. 6 (1998): 35; Bruce Rubenstein, "Ethics and Compliance Officers Meet to Share Information and Best Practices," *Corporate Legal Times*, 10, no. 99 (2000): 72.

5. Dove Izraeli and Anat BarNir, "Promoting Ethics through Ethics Officers: A Proposed Profile and an Application," *Journal of Business Ethics*, 17, no. 11 (1998): 1189–1196.

6. Luis R. Gomez-Mejia, David B. Balkin, and Robert L. Cardy, "Developing an Effective Whistle-Blowing Policy," included in *Managing Human Resources*, 5th edition (Upper Saddle River, NJ: Pearson Prentice Hall, 2007): 451.

7. www.ombudsassociation.org, accessed 9/16/08.

8. Larry B. Hill, "The Ombudsman Revisited: Thirty Years of Hawaiian Experience," *Public Administration Review*, 62, no. 1 (2002): 24–41.

9. www.putnam.com/ombudsman, accessed 9/16/08.

10. www.aicpa.org/professional+resources/professional+ethics+ code+of+professional+conduct/professional+ethics/, accessed 9/16/08.

11. Anonymous, "Extolling the Virtues of Hot Lines," *Workforce*, 77, no. 6 (1998): 125–126.

12. www.ethicspoint.com, accessed 9/16/08.

13. Richard De George, "Ethical Responsibilities of Engineers in Large Organizations," *Business & Professional Ethics Journal*, 1, no. 1 (1981): 1–14.

14. Robin Page West, "Employment Law: How a Qui Tam Whistleblower Case Works," July 1999, available at www.

expertlaw.com/library/employment/qui-tam.html, accessed 9/16/08.; see also www.ouitamonline.com, accessed 9/16/08.

15. www.taf.org/top100fca.htm, accessed 9/16/08.

16. www.taf.org/whistleblower.htm, accessed 9/16/08.

17. Sarbanes-Oxley Act of 2002, "Protection for Employees of Publicly Traded Companies who Provide Evidence of Fraud," H.R. 3763, Section 806: 58–60; available at http://fl1.findlaw.com/news.findlaw.com/hdocs/docs/gwbush/sarbanesoxley072302.pdf, accessed 9/15/08.

18. Stephen Taub, "SEC: 1300 'Whistles' Blow Each Day: Most Tips Concerning Accounting Problems at Public Companies," *CFO.com*, August 3, 2004.

19. Thomas L. Carson, Mary Ellen Verdu, and Richard E. Wokutch, "Whistle-Blowing for Profit: An Ethical Analysis of the Federal False Claims Act," *Journal of Business Ethics*, 77, no. 3 (2008): 361–376.

20. Cynthia Cooper, *Extraordinary Circumstances* (Hoboken, NJ: John Wiley & Sons, 2008).

CHAPTER 9

Ethical Leadership, Work Goals, and Performance Appraisals

After reading this chapter, you will be able to:

- Describe how managers are ethical role models
- Set work goals using management-by-objectives
- Implement stress reduction techniques
- Design and conduct performance appraisals that encourage ethical behavior
- Effectively and fairly discipline employees for work rule violations

Why might a usually ethical employee decide to suddenly mislead a manager or customer about meeting an end-of-the-month product delivery deadline? When questioned, one might expect to hear the employee claim that he or she was under pressure and rationalize that:

> . . . my boss sometimes does it!

> . . . I had to meet my monthly work goal!

> . . . it counts a lot in my monthly performance review!

Three aspects of daily organizational life significantly impact an employee's ethical performance:

1. The direct supervisor's behaviors

2. Work goals

3. Performance appraisals

This chapter explores how managers are ethical role models, how to establish work goals that encourage ethical behavior, and how to create performance appraisals that reward ethical behaviors.

Managers as Ethical Role Models

Managers are role models, and the ethics of their actions are constantly being evaluated by subordinates. Actions speak louder than words; the way a manager treats owners, customers, and employees sets the standard for acceptable behavior within the manager's work unit. A manager's behavioral commitment to ethical principles, or lack thereof, filters down to subordinates and other employees. Managers have already been promoted, so their daily workplace actions are indicators to subordinates of what it takes to be promoted.

Hard-working, conscientious, caring, and moral managers who generate high-quality performance outcomes tend to attract, develop, and promote hard-working, conscientious, caring, and moral employees who generate high-quality performance outcomes.

On the other hand, if a manager comes in late, leaves early, performs shoddy work, violates confidentiality, and cuts ethical corners to achieve work goals, then so will the manager's subordinates, particularly when the manager is not around.

Direct supervisors have the greatest impact on an employee's ethical performance by modeling acceptable behavior through daily interactions, determining work goals, and conducting performance appraisals. Throughout this chapter, "supervisor" refers to the person an employee reports to, whether the head of production, a middle manager, or the CEO.

According to a recent study of employees, a significant percentage of their managers are ethically challenged.[1] Among the survey respondents:

- 39% reported that their managers failed to keep promises.

- 37% reported that their managers failed to give credit when due.

- 24% reported that their managers violated employee privacy.

- 23% reported that their managers blamed others to cover up mistakes or to minimize embarrassment.

These managerial misbehaviors contradict the attribute employees most want their leaders and supervisors to exhibit—honesty.[2] Honesty is a mutually reinforcing ethical bond between managers and their subordinates. Dishonesty by either the manager or employees punctures the ethics bond between them.

A highly ethical employee receiving daily direction from a dishonest supervisor will deal with the stress by loyally aligning with the supervisor's dishonest methods, disloyally going behind the supervisor's back, or quitting.

Great Place to Work® Dimensions

The Great Place to Work® Institute provides a model of best management practices for creating a work culture that achieves superior performance. The Institute surveys employees and encourages organizations to benchmark against each other and their own previous performance.[3] The survey results form the basis of *Fortune* magazine's annual list of 100 Best Companies to Work For.

A great place to work is defined by the Institute as a place where people "trust the people they work for, have pride in what they do, and enjoy the people they work with."[4] Such an organization has high levels of credibility, respect, fairness, pride, and camaraderie. Exhibit 9.1 summarizes how the model's five dimensions are exemplified.[5]

EXHIBIT 9.1

Great Place to Work® Dimensions

Dimension	How It Plays Out in the Workplace
Credibility	• Communications are open and accessible • Competence in coordinating human and material resources • Integrity in carrying out vision with consistency

Respect	• Support professional development and show appreciation • Collaborate with employees on relevant decisions • Care for employees as individuals with personal lives
Fairness	• Equity: balanced treatment for all in terms of rewards • Impartiality: absence of favoritism in hiring and promotions • Justice: lack of discrimination and process for appeals
Pride	• In personal job, individual contributions • In work produced by one's team or work group • In the organization's products and standing in the community
Camaraderie	• Ability to be oneself • Socially friendly and welcoming atmosphere • Sense of "family" or "team"

Similar to research on ethical organizations, researchers report that these great workplaces receive more qualified job applicants, have lower levels of turnover and lower healthcare costs, and have higher levels of customer satisfaction, productivity, and profitability.

Virtues and Leadership Practices

Managers can possess an infinite number of virtues, and can expect the same of their subordinates. The top seven desired virtues are:

1. Mission-driven

2. Honest

3. Fair

4. Supportive

5. Respectful

6. Quality-focused

7. Accountable

These virtues serve as the ethical foundation for leadership practices in organizations that achieve superior performance. Jack Welch, the former CEO of General Electric, notes that although successful leaders may have very different personalities—compare Microsoft's introspective Bill Gates to Southwest Airlines' exuberant Herb Kelleher—they tend to have eight management practices in common. Successful leaders:[6]

1. Relentlessly upgrade their team, using every encounter as an opportunity to evaluate, coach, and build self-confidence.

2. Make sure people not only see the vision, they live and breathe it.

3. Get into everyone's skin, exuding positive energy and optimism.

4. Establish trust with candor, transparency, and credit.

5. Have the courage, after listening, to make unpopular decisions and gut calls.

6. Probe and push with a curiosity that borders on skepticism, making sure their questions are answered with action.

7. Take risks, learn from their mistakes, and inspire others to do likewise.

8. Celebrate organizational and employee accomplishments.

One of the greatest challenges for supervisors is to acknowledge and accept their own failures as well as that of their subordinates. Failure becomes the foundation for success when lessons learned from the failure inform the next effort.

Work Goals

Work goals can generate unethical behaviors. Stretch goals sometimes tempt employees to stretch the truth. According to research, people close to achieving a difficult goal are very tempted to behave unethically if that is the only way they can achieve the goal by the specified deadline.[7]

Unreasonable production outcome goals, for instance, can influence some supervisors to conduct inadequate product quality verifications and bankers to approve very risky loans they normally would reject.

Sales performance goals are a particularly troublesome area. Researchers report that 79% of surveyed managers have heard salespeople make an unrealistic promise on sales calls.[8] In *The Force*, David Dorsey shadowed the top salesperson at Xerox.[9] To be rewarded for accomplishing 120% of his sales goal, this otherwise relatively nice salesperson regularly lies about product price and capabilities, his negotiating authority, his work schedule, the availability of customer perks, and product delivery capabilities. He did whatever it took to close a deal, which usually meant lying and being manipulative.

Senior Arthur Andersen partners overseeing the Enron account had to wrestle with the tension between achieving very difficult financial performance goals and their professional obligations (see *In the Real World: Auditor Oversight Problems—Spring 2001*). Enron was a $50 million account and the lead auditor's annual bonus was contingent on increasing these fees by 20%.

Auditor Oversight Problems—Spring 2001

Enron's Board of Directors decided to exempt Andy Fastow from the Code of Ethics policy. LJM1, however, violated Generally Accepted Accounting Principles because the SPE's management team was not independent of Enron. This technicality was lost amongst the flurry of mergers and acquisitions demanding the Board's attention. Fastow's management of LJM1, and its well-hidden purchases of Enron's assets, enabled Enron to meet quarterly financial targets.

Fastow's creative financing efforts were widely acclaimed in the business media, earning him *CFO Magazine's* 1999 CFO Excellence Award. Enron's 1999 revenue reached $40 billion, a very impressive 28% increase from the previous year, and $100 billion for 2000. Enron climbed to #7 on the Fortune 500 list and was now the nation's largest supplier of electricity, as well as natural gas.

Enron became the hottest stock on Wall Street. Stock purchased in March 1997 for $40, when Jeff Skilling became COO, achieved a stock-split adjusted value of $181 a share in August 2000. In 2000, Enron won *Fortune* magazine's most innovative company award for the fifth consecutive year and was ranked #25 for "Most Admired Company in the World."

In the midst of these accolades, Ken Lay triumphantly retired as Enron's CEO in February 2001, passing the reins on to Skilling, his protégé. The succession plan included Skilling taking over for Lay as Enron's Chairman of the Board of Directors at the end of 2001.

Meanwhile, within Arthur Andersen, Carl Bass was promoted to the company's Professional Standards Group (PSG), an oversight team composed of experienced senior partners who provide independent rulings on contentious accounting issues for audit teams. The Enron account fell under Bass's jurisdiction. In the spring of 2001, Bass refused to sign off on a questionable financial structure for a series of Fastow-created SPEs. Bass instructed David Duncan, the Andersen audit team's lead accountant, to inform Enron's Board of Directors about the SPE accounting problem.

Duncan ignored Bass's order and shared the problem with Rick Causey, Enron's CAO and former Andersen partner. Causey, incensed by what he considered to be Bass's unfair treatment, complained bitterly to senior Arthur Andersen partners. Causey and other Enron executives threatened to change audit companies if Bass was not removed from the Enron account and replaced by a different PSG member. The Enron account earned a remarkable $50 million in fees for Arthur Andersen's Houston office.

DECISION CHOICE. If you were a senior Arthur Andersen partner, and Enron strongly requested that Carl Bass be replaced by a different Professional Standards Group (PSG) member to review Duncan's audit team's work, would you:

❶ Defend Bass and risk losing the $50 million Enron account?

❷ Remove Bass from the Enron account and replace him with another highly qualified PSG member?

Why?

Goal Setting

Work goals are a very powerful management tool for driving behaviors and must be carefully formulated. Depending on the nature of the job task, establish daily, weekly, monthly, and yearly goals. In addition, establish and review interim goals, and reward employees for achieving them.

SMART goals exhibit five aspects. The acronym stands for goals that are:[10]

1. *Specific*—The outcome is clearly identifiable.

2. *Measurable*—The outcome can be measured.

3. *Aligned*—The outcome contributes to organizational strategy.

4. *Reachable*—The outcome is challenging, but realistically attainable.

5. *Time-Bound*—The outcome is to be achieved by a specific point in time.

"Doing Your Best" is an inadequate employee goal. "Best" needs to be clearly defined, such as increasing sales by 5% by December 31. A clearly defined goal statement that meets the five SMART criteria minimizes ambiguity about employee performance expectations.

Managers should require that employees provide input to ensure that the goals are attainable. Often, if asked to determine a "fair" goal, employees offer goals that are equal to, or more difficult than, goals managers would initially propose. Employee participation in the goal-setting process increases their commitment and accountability to the goal. Establishing feedback sessions to review goal progress also increases the likelihood of success.

Management-By-Objectives

Management-by-objectives (MBO) is a goal-setting technique in which managers and their subordinates jointly determine work unit and individual goals in alignment with organizational goals.

The MBO process begins with executives defining the organization's strategic goals in ways that are specific and measurable. These goals are then cascaded downward through the organization. The next level of managers, be it a division or department, meet to establish goals that are in alignment with the organization's strategic goals. Then members of the manager's work unit meet to establish goals that are in alignment with department goals.

Lastly, employees meet with their supervisor to develop individual goals in alignment with the work unit's goals. Jointly review the employee's previous performance, as well as the performances of others with similar job tasks, to determine a goal range. Then have the employee propose a challenging, yet attainable, goal within this range, along with strategies that will lead to goal achievement.

The supervisor can accept the employee's goal, maintain that the goal is too difficult, or challenge the employee to propose a more difficult goal. If one of the latter two cases occurs, jointly develop a more appropriate goal and discuss strategies for goal achievement.

Stress Management

Goals require deadlines, and deadlines can create stress through psychological and physical tension. High levels of stress, inappropriately managed, can lead to health problems, low productivity, accidents, absenteeism, turnover, and unethical employee behaviors.[11]

Work goals are just one source of workplace stress. Other causes of stress include conflicts at work, rapid change, unfavorable working conditions, autocratic or incompetent supervisors, and personal problems at home.

Organizations can help employees manage stress through wellness programs, employee assistance programs, delegation training, time-management training, quiet time, and meditation.

Wellness Programs

Wellness programs contain a menu of health-related opportunities, including physical fitness and exercising, smoking cessation, and nutrition management. Some organizations provide their own fitness centers that are open 24 hours a day, though most organizations contract out to local health centers.

Employee Assistance Programs (EAPs)

EAPs were initially created for employees experiencing drug and alcohol abuse. They have been expanded to include financial planning, depression, and family care issues. An employee's participation in an EAP is typically confidential information, as are any issues discussed with a professional consultant.

Delegation Training

Sometimes stress is caused by employees taking on too many responsibilities. Delegation training helps employees establish priorities. Employees need to understand what activities they must perform, and what activities can be performed by other employees. Too much delegation, on the other hand, can increase everyone else's stress level.

Time-Management Training

Employees can also feel overwhelmed because they are not well-organized or must respond to a never-ending litany of crises. Employees should conduct a time analysis of work activities during the course of a week, and then set priorities to be more in control of their daily work life.

Quiet Time

Some organizations designate a specific time period where employees can perform job tasks without being interrupted by phone calls, urgent meetings, e-mail communications, or other pressing matters.[12] Quiet time can be a particular hour every week, or several hours spread across the work week. After quiet time ends, the employee is once again available for contact.

Meditation

Sometimes employees need to step back from daily work demands and simply relax. Meditation is an excellent form of relaxation and, with practice, can be successfully conducted within 12 minutes. Meditation helps a person develop clarity of mind and patience. Organizations such as Apple Computer, McKinsey Consulting, Hughes Aircraft, and Google offer meditation as an employee benefit.

Managers can meditate on their own or lead members of their work unit in a meditation session held in a conference room. The process is rather simple:[13]

Step 1: Find a quiet place where you will not be disturbed.

Step 2: Set a timer with a soft bell for the desired length of the session.

Step 3: Sit up straight on the floor with legs crossed in a lotus position, or on a chair with your feet firmly on the ground.

Step 4: Slowly relax your muscles.

Step 5: Close your eyes and breathe slowly in a regular rhythm. If a beginner, start by counting breaths. Inhale, momentarily hold the breath, and count the exhale as "one." Continue counting upward to a specific number, such as 40. If the number of a particular breath is forgotten, just begin counting again. More experienced meditators focus on the blank space within one's consciousness or chant. A poetic Buddhist chant is:

> Inhale #1: "Breathe in, I calm my body."
> Exhale #1: "Breathe out, I smile."
> Inhale #2: "Dwelling in the present moment,"
> Exhale #2: "I know that it is a wonderful moment."

Step 6: Breathe each breath slightly deeper and hold slightly longer.

Step 7: Distracting thoughts will enter your mind. Don't engage the thought, let it go. If you fear losing a vital thought, just write it down on a nearby piece of paper and then resume the meditation process.

Step 8: Continue the process until the alarm gently sounds. Slowly become aware of where you are, open your eyes, and get up gradually.

Performance Appraisals

Performance appraisals should help employees become better people. The performance evaluation serves as an employee scorecard.

Employees are more likely to pay attention to an issue if it is included on the scorecard.

Performance appraisals should document employee accomplishments and benchmark the distance an employee still needs to travel to become an ideal employee. Link performance appraisal results to merit raises and promotions to ensure that employees who behave ethically, and achieve goals in alignment with organizational objectives, are appropriately rewarded.

Poorly managed performance appraisals are detrimental to employee morale and productivity. Some managers do not conduct timely performance evaluations, give poor performers average ratings to avoid conflict, give excellent performers average ratings for political reasons, or apply subjective criteria such as favoritism rather than objective performance measures.

Design performance appraisals, and gather relevant data, that address four ethical performance issues:

1. Does the employee behave unethically?

2. Does the employee live up to the code of ethics?

3. Does the employee embody the attitudes and behaviors of an ideal employee?

4. Does the employee achieve and support ethics-based initiatives?

These performance appraisal measures are discussed in the following sections.

"Unethical Behavior" Self-Assessment Performance Appraisals

Socrates said, "To thine own self be true." Nobody is ethically perfect, yet people tend to resist sharing their imperfections with others. Have employees conduct a very honest, and confidential, self-assessment of their own struggles to behave ethically at work.

Begin by developing a list of unethical behaviors employees have observed at work. This can be fun to develop. Then create a short survey where employees confidentially self-assess how often they behave this way. Items might include:[14]

- I misrepresent facts about my job activities to my boss and co-workers.
- I divulge personal or confidential information.
- I permit, or fail to report, law violations or thefts.
- I take credit for other people's ideas.

The survey reinforces that these unethical behaviors are wrong and provides the employee with ethical performance goals for the next appraisal period.

Living Up to the Code of Ethics Performance Appraisals

Annually appraise how well employees perform according to the organization's Code of Ethics. In Chapter 4, an organization's five-item Code of Ethics (see Exhibit 4.3) was transformed into an organizational assessment survey to benchmark progress (see Exhibit 4.4). The survey has been modified in Exhibit 9.2 for the purpose of conducting an individualized performance appraisal.

EXHIBIT 9.2

Code of Ethics Performance Appraisal

Instructions: Please use the 1–5 scale below to assess how well each of the following statements exemplifies the employee's performance:

1 = *Strongly Disagree;* 2 = *Disagree;* 3 = *Neither Agree nor Disagree;* 4 = *Agree;* 5 = *Strongly Agree*

	SD	D	N	A	SA
Operates with integrity and respect	1	2	3	4	5
Provides and promotes Legendary Service (meets and exceeds customer expectations)	1	2	3	4	5
Uses superior communications (is professional, courteous, and prompt)	1	2	3	4	5
Embraces continuous improvement (becomes more productive and efficient)	1	2	3	4	5
Actively engages in self-management (assesses performance daily)	1	2	3	4	5

Total Score of Items Above:

Which of these items should the employee improve upon between now and the next performance review?

How can the employee score higher on that item?

Ideal Employee Attitudes and Behaviors Performance Appraisals

Annually appraise employee performance based on the qualities of an ideal employee. Chapter 6 provides a "Qualities of an Ideal Employee" survey (see Exhibit 6.7) developed by a team of managers for their subordinates. The seven factors, each operationalized with behavioral descriptors, are: general character, customer relations, colleague relations, communication skills, work task skills, continuous improvement, and company pride.

Develop ideal profiles for every category of employee—executives, managers, supervisors, and subordinates—and appraise accordingly. Exhibit 9.3 is a sample survey.[15]

EXHIBIT 9.3

Leadership Skills Performance Appraisal

Instructions: Please use the 1–4 scale below to assess how well each of the following statements exemplifies the employee's performance:

4 = Always; 3 = Frequently; 2 = Sometimes; 1 = Never

	Rating			
	A	F	S	N
Is positive	4	3	2	1
Listens well	4	3	2	1
Is comfortable giving feedback	4	3	2	1
Is trusted by others	4	3	2	1
Is easy to approach	4	3	2	1
Is available to others when needed	4	3	2	1
Communicates clearly	4	3	2	1
Seeks input from others	4	3	2	1
Praises others	4	3	2	1
Is patient	4	3	2	1
Follows through on commitments	4	3	2	1

Is supportive	4	3	2	1
Provides clear expectations	4	3	2	1
Knows others well	4	3	2	1

Total Score of Items Above:

Which of these items should the employee improve upon between now and the next performance review?

How can the employee score higher on that item?

Ethics-Based Initiatives Performance Appraisals

Appraise employee performance for all ethics-based initiatives. These items may include affirmative action hiring and promotion goals, work unit ethics scores, percentage of employees participating in ethics and diversity training workshops, theft reductions, and number of employee grievances.

Collection and Evaluation Issues

How performance appraisal information is collected and evaluated raises ethical issues. Collect the information from a wide range of people who interact with the person being evaluated, not just from the direct supervisor. In addition, use a rating system, rather than a ranking system, to evaluate the data.

360-Degree Performance Evaluations

Most direct supervisors observe only a small portion of an employee's performance. An employee may behave admirably in the presence of the direct supervisor, but inadequately when not closely monitored.

Whenever feasible, conduct 360-degree performance evalua-tions.[16] Many Web-based systems make this previously onerous pro-cess easy to complete, tabulate, and put into report format.

To achieve a holistic perspective of the employee, have the employee, the supervisor, peers, and employee's direct reports com-plete the performance evaluation. When appropriate, obtain evalua-tions from customers and suppliers.

Keep individual responses confidential. Respondents are more likely to provide critical feedback if ratings and comments cannot be traced back to the respondent. Otherwise, respondents will be tempted to inflate their scores to avoid future conflict with, or retali-ation from, the person being evaluated.

Out of respect for the person being evaluated, keep individual performance evaluation results confidential unless the employee in-sists that they be made public. Vineet Nayar, CEO of HCT Technol-ogies, demonstrated a high degree of vulnerability, transparency, and trust in his employees by publishing his own 360-degree perform-ance evaluation results on a company Intranet site.[17]

Rating versus Ranking

Employees can be rated in comparison to an absolute standard of per-formance or ranked in comparison to each other. A rating system is more ethical than a ranking system. Ranking creates unhealthy com-petition among employees and may not adequately describe an employee's value to the work unit.

If only one employee in a work unit can receive the #1 ranking, for instance, employees in the work unit will be tempted to compete, rather than cooperate, with each other to achieve the highest rank. Why help a colleague if doing so might result in the colleague being ranked higher than you?

Conversely, one employee must receive the lowest rank in a work unit composed of highly talented and well-trained employees. Technically, the employee is the worst performer in the group. But, the employee is still a very good performer. Falsely labeling a very good performer as the worst performer can damage work unit morale and be very detrimental to the employee's career within the organization.

Performance Appraisal Feedback

The purpose of a performance appraisal feedback session is to praise an employee's good behaviors and accomplishments and develop strategies for improving weaknesses. Performance appraisal feedback sessions can be very tense. Carefully manage the feedback session, because employees may feel anxious about giving or receiving critical information.

On a regular basis, provide positive feedback immediately after a praiseworthy behavior and constructive feedback immediately after a blameworthy behavior. Employees who informally receive feedback on a regular basis are less surprised by the annual formal performance appraisal results and better prepared to discuss improvement issues.

Meet personally with each direct report to discuss the performance appraisal results. Hold performance appraisal feedback sessions in a neutral setting, such as a conference room. Conducting appraisal feedback sessions in the supervisor's office, particularly if the feedback is critical, creates an uncomfortable office environment.

Employees may avoid visiting a supervisor's office because of the negative memories associated with performance evaluations.

Prior to the meeting, compare the employee's self-assessment with the 360-degree performance appraisal results. Begin the meeting by discussing those areas that both the employee and the raters highlighted as strengths. Praise these behaviors and accomplishments.

Then discuss any areas raters highlighted as strengths but the employee did not. Make the employee aware that others are impressed with these behaviors and outcomes. Next, discuss any areas the employee highlighted as strengths but the raters did not. Explore with the employee why this perceptual gap exists.

Lastly, discuss those areas that both the employee and raters highlighted as weaknesses. Focus on solving the problem and how to improve the weakness. Jointly establish goals and strategies that will likely lead to better results.

Disciplining Work Rule Violations

Some previously unknown employee work rule violations may be revealed by the 360-degree performance appraisal process. Punishments, as well as rewards, influence employee performance. Unethical behaviors must be punished.

Fairness is an extremely important ethical value in all organizations. How managers respond to allegations that a subordinate has behaved unethically significantly influences how employees evaluate a manager's fairness.

Everyone is innocent until proven guilty. Investigate the situation prior to imposing disciplinary action. Maybe the employee's behavior was misunderstood by the respondent or justifiable given additional contextual information.

Major Infractions

Employees define major and minor ethical infractions based on the type of punishment determined by managers. Any behavior punished harshly is considered a major infraction and gets the attention of employees. Employee theft and drug and alcohol violations are typically treated as major ethical infractions.

Polygraph tests can be used for employee theft. Managers must have good cause before submitting an employee to a polygraph test. Otherwise, trust is being violated and employee morale will suffer. Exhibit 9.4 summarizes some key rules governing employee polygraph tests.[18]

EXHIBIT 9.4

Employee Polygraph Protection Act of 1988

Key factors of the legislation include:

- Random polygraph testing of employees is prohibited.

- Polygraphs can be used on employees who are reasonably suspected of involvement in a specific workplace incident resulting in economic loss to the employer.

- An employee can refuse to take the polygraph test or terminate a polygraph test at any time; refusal for not participating in a polygraph test cannot be used as a reason for discipline or job termination.

- If an employee fails the polygraph test, the employee cannot be fired without other corroborating evidence.

Violations of drug and alcohol rules are also major ethical infractions. Randomly test employees whose activities continually put public safety at risk for alcohol abuse and drug use. Chapter 3 summarizes some key elements of alcohol and drug testing.

Minor Infractions

Many workplace violations are relatively minor, such as being late for work or playing solitaire on the computer during work time. Constructively address minor infractions before they escalate into bigger problems.

The following is a continuum of potential punishments, beginning with the most lenient and ending with the harshest, for managing workplace violations.[19]

1. Talk to, and coach, the employee about the problem
2. Oral warning
3. Written warning
4. Provide special in-house services to help employee
5. Send employee to formal training to help
6. Explore transferring employee to a different department
7. Put the employee on probation
8. Fine the employee or withhold portion of merit pay
9. Suspend without pay
10. Termination

The goal of discipline is to rehabilitate employees who violate work rules, not to fire them. Guilty parties should acknowledge the wrongdoing, apologize, and then change behavior. Effective rehabilitation also requires that the employee being disciplined accepts the fairness of the disciplinary process. Termination is appropriate if rehabilitation fails or the violation is severe.

Forgiveness

Management and nonmanagement employees will make mistakes, and their words and behaviors may harm others. Managers must exemplify the value of forgiveness and coach employees on how to forgive. This is particularly important if the work group is recovering from a dishonest or abusive manager. The previous manager's dishonest or abusive behaviors are likely to be projected on the new manager. The new manager should acknowledge and heal the harm caused by the previous manager, rather than ignore the harm.

Robert Enright defines forgiveness as a gift freely given in the face of moral wrong, without denying the wrong itself.[20] Forgiveness recognizes the inherent worth of the wrongdoer and replaces resentment the violated person may feel with goodwill, a process that increases the forgiver's self-esteem.

Enright offers a four-phase model that managers can apply to guide employees through the forgiveness process.

Phase 1: Uncovering Phase: The violated person recognizes that the unjust situation has created unhealthy anger and emotional pain.

Phase 2: Decision Phase: The violated person explores the personal pain or damage that would continue by not forgiving the wrongdoer, compared to the positive changes that could occur by forgiving.

Phase 3: Work Phase: The violated person grieves over the unfairness of the wrongdoing, reframes the wrongdoer as a person of inherent human worth deserving of forgiveness, and practices the virtues of goodness, service, mercy, and generosity by forgiving the wrongdoer.

Phase 4: Outcome Phase: The forgiving person experiences the emotionally healing benefits of forgiveness and finds meaning in the previous suffering.

Summary

Managers must clearly signal on a daily basis that ethical behavior is expected, and unethical behavior is unacceptable. Employees learn more about what types of behaviors are acceptable by observing the actions of their direct supervisors, rather than from listening to inspirational words coming out of the executive suite.

Work goals and performance appraisals also influence ethical expectations and performance on a daily basis. Establish work goals that inspire ethical behavior. Beware of stretch goals that may tempt employees to stretch the truth about performance.

Formally appraise the employee's ethical performance on an annual basis and link these scores to merit raises and promotions. Address any work rule violations immediately and fairly. Even if the wrongdoer is terminated, psychologically heal the workforce and redevelop a culture of trust by helping employees forgive the wrongdoer.

Notes

1. Paul Harvey, Jason Stoner, Wayne Hochwater, and Charles Kacmar, "Coping with Abusive Supervision: The Neutralizing Effects of Ingratiation and Positive Affect on Negative Employee Outcomes," *The Leadership Quarterly*, 18, no. 3 (2007): 264–280.

2. James M. Kouzes and Barry Z. Posner, *The Leadership Challenge*, 4th edition (Hoboken, NJ: John Wiley & Sons, 2007).

3. www.greatplacetowork.com, accessed 9/18/08.

4. www.greatplacetowork.com/great/model.php, accessed 9/18/08.

5. www.greatplacetowork.com/great/dimensions.php, accessed 9/18/08.

6. Jack Welch and Suzy Welch, WINNING (New York: HarperBusiness, 2002).

7. Maurice E. Schweitzer, Lisa Ordonez, and Bambi Douma, "The Role of Goal Setting in Motivating Unethical Behavior," *Academy of Management Journal*, 47, no. 3 (2004): 422–432.

8. Erin Stout, "To Tell the Truth," *Sales & Marketing Management*, 154, no. 7 (2002): 40+.

9. David Dorsey, *The Force* (New York: Random House, 1994).

10. Edwin A. Locke and Gary Latham, *A Theory of Goal Setting and Task Performance* (Upper Saddle River, NJ: Prentice Hall, 1990).

11. Wendell L. French, *Human Resources Management*, 6th edition (New York: Houghton Mifflin Company, 2007): 512; see also www.stress.org/job.htm, accessed 9/18/08.

12. Kirk Ladendorf, "Intel Tries Out Some Quiet Time in Austin," *American Statesman*, July 21, 2008.

13. Sylvia Boorstein, *Don't Just Do Something, Sit There* (New York: HarperOne, 1996).

14. See sample survey in Sharon Lund O'Neil and Elwood N. Chapman, *Your Attitude is Showing*, 12th edition (Upper Saddle River, NJ: Pearson Prentice Hall, 2008): 249.

15. Modified from Chris Clarke-Epstein, *78 Important Questions Every Leader Should Ask and Answer* (New York: Amacom, 2006).

16. Jeffrey I. Seglin, "Reviewing Your Boss," *Fortune*, June 11, 2001: 248.

17. Jena McGregor, "The Employee is Always Right," *Business Week*, November 19, 2007: 80–82.

18. www.dol.gov/esa/whd/regs/statutes/poly01.pdf, accessed 9/18/08.

19. Jerald Greenberg and Robert A. Baron, *Behavior in Organizations*, 9th edition (Upper Saddle River, NJ: Pearson Prentice Hall, 2008): 124.

20. Robert D. Enright, *Forgiveness is a Choice* (Washington, D.C.: APA Books, 2001); see also www.forgiveness-institute.org, accessed 9/18/08.

CHAPTER 10

Empowering Ethical Employees

After reading this chapter, you will be able to:

- Empower three types of employees: go-getters, fence-sitters, and adversarials
- Create effective problem-solving teams
- Conduct an Appreciative Inquiry workshop to achieve superior customer service
- Implement a Scanlon-type gainsharing plan and Open Book Management
- Distribute financial improvements to all employees through profit sharing, stock options, Employee Stock Ownership Plans, and Cooperatives

An ethical organization is a community of people in which every employee has a sense of organizational ownership and accountability. All employees should be empowered to control their immediate surroundings and have the freedom and authority to do what needs to get done.

Some systems of management treat nonmanagement employees with greater respect than others by actively involving them in the decision-making process. Researchers report that top-down, one-way communication and decision-making processes make subordinates passive and reactive, rather than proactive, and have a detrimental effect on an employee's moral development.[1]

This chapter explores ways to create a fully empowered workforce in which employees effectively participate on teams, develop plans for superior customer service and continuous improvement, and share in the financial benefits generated by their efforts.

Go-Getters, Fence-Sitters, and Adversarials

Being ethical and fair does not mean all employees must be treated exactly the same. Each employee has different capabilities and attitudes toward work. Different types of employees require different types of motivation and leadership.

Some managers mistakenly design systems to control the worst employees and, in the name of fairness, impose the same control system on all employees. When this happens, some of the best employees quit for employment with an organization that will treat them with the respect they deserve. Managers should treat their best employees differently than other employees—they have earned it.

Most organizations have three types of employees in terms of workplace attitudes and behaviors:[2]

1. Go-getters, who are fully engaged with the work experience

2. Fence-sitters, who put in a good day's work for a good day's pay

3. Adversarials, who have a bad attitude to both the nature of work and authority

Organizations of high integrity and superior performance are able to attract and retain a large number of go-getters. The average organization, however, typically consists of a handful of go-getters, many fence-sitters, and a handful of adversarial employees. Managers must treat the three employee groups differently.

Exhibit 10.1 summarizes these three types of employees.

EXHIBIT 10.1

Workplace Attitudes and Behaviors

Type	Prevalence	Attitude and Behavior	How to Manage
Go-getters	Some	Task-oriented Can-do Enjoys working	Provide freedom and autonomy Give new challenges Develop for leadership positions Praise and offer extra rewards
Fence-sitters	Many	A job is a job Minimum expectations 9–5, then punch out	Raise minimum expectations Team up with go-getters Separate from adversarials
Adversarials	Some	Managers are idiots Work is a pain Convert fence-sitters	Confront and discipline Team up with go-getters Separate from fence-sitters

Go-Getters

Go-getters are task-oriented employees with a "can-do" attitude. They enjoy working, are proactive, and appreciate new challenges. They tend to be exemplary organizational citizens. Go-getters are satisfied with their jobs, deeply involved with their work, trust supervisors, and perceive fairness in organizational procedures and outcomes.[3] They have plenty of ideas for continuous improvement and want the freedom to implement their creative solutions.

Groom go-getters for leadership positions. Go-getters prefer to work on their own or with other go-getters. They find fence-sitters uninspired and adversarial employees juvenile. Challenge go-getters to work with fence-sitters and adversarial employees. Go-getters can teach fence-sitters easier ways to perform their work tasks. Go-getters can offer adversarial employees a more constructive way to frame organizational events and apply their energy.

Fence-Sitters

Fence-sitters meet managerial expectations and go no further. They do not try to self-actualize through work, like go-getters. A job is a necessary burden to pay expenses. Enjoyment is to be experienced outside work hours, not during work hours. They tolerate managers because they do not want to be fired. Fence-sitters watch the clock and count down the minutes until departure.

Challenge fence-sitters by continually raising performance expectations. The more that is expected of fence-sitters, the more they will accomplish. Go-getters can show fence-sitters how to effectively and efficiently achieve results. Separate fence-sitters from adversarial employees, who typically try to distract fence-sitters from putting in a good day's work.

Adversarial Employees

Adversarial employees do not like work and possess negative attitudes toward others, particularly managers and go-getters. They often slack off when not under managerial observation and encourage fence-sitters to do likewise. They view managers as the enemy and criticize managers every chance they can get. Adversarial employees find creative ways to leave work early, and then brag about it to each other and the fence-sitters.

Confront and discipline adversarial employees. Otherwise, they will not change their attitudes or behaviors. Sometimes an employee is adversarial because the job fit is inappropriate. In that case, assign the adversarial employee to a different task, workgroup, or manager. Require that adversarial employees receive counseling through the organization's EAP program to get at the root of their negative work attitude, which may be grounded in childhood experiences.

Closely supervise adversarial employees, because they cannot be trusted to act with the organization's best interests at heart. Document the behavioral impacts of their negative attitudes, such as failure to cooperate with managers or go-getters. Give adversarial employees an opportunity to change by a jointly determined deadline and dismiss them if the agreed-upon change does not occur.

Sometimes an adversarial employee needs more, not less, freedom. The adversarial employee can be rebelling against having been overly controlled. Within clearly defined parameters, managers should experiment by giving an adversarial employee more responsibility and see what happens. If the adversarial employee does not respond as hoped for, quickly end the experiment.

Some adversarial employees, when they do change, can become go-getters. Adversarial employees have leadership skills, though they are directed toward the wrong ends. Some reformed adversarial employees are very grateful for being given another chance.

In the Real World: Informing Ken Lay—August 2001 highlights the tension between Enron's Sherron Watkins, who in this case was an ethical go-getter, and corporate lawyers, who may have been either ethical fence-sitters or adversarials.

IN THE REAL WORLD

Informing Ken Lay—August 2001

At Enron's request, Arthur Andersen's senior partners removed Carl Bass from reviewing the Enron account and reassigned him to SEC relations. Unfortunately, in 2000 the Internet economic bubble burst, the nation entered into a recession, and the stock market declined. For Enron, this meant losing many Internet customers and being financially overextended when the credit markets tightened. Negative publicity associated with Enron traders manipulating the California electricity trading market didn't help.

Nonetheless, Enron claimed $100 billion in revenue for the first half of 2001 and stock analysts estimated that at this pace Enron would end the year as #1 on the Fortune 500 list.

But then a subset of Andy Fastow's network of SPEs began to collapse because they were funded primarily with Enron stock, which was declining in value with the rest of the stock market. Fastow's conflict of interest became more apparent. Skilling ordered Fastow to resign either from Enron or as LJM's managing partner. Fastow decided to remain as Enron's CFO. Instead, Michael Kopper, Fastow's assistant and protégé, resigned from Enron and took over as LJM's managing partner.

The pressure was getting to Skilling as his dream job started to turn into a financial nightmare. If Enron's stock continued to decline in price, more Fastow-created SPEs would collapse. He struggled with depression, alcohol consumption, and insomnia. On August 13, 2001, Skilling shocked the Board of Directors by submitting his resignation as Enron's CEO, due to family reasons. The public announcement resulted in a massive sell-off of Enron stock, and its price plummeted.

Ken Lay agreed to come out of semi-retirement to serve as Enron's CEO again and re-establish stock market confidence. He announced an all-employee meeting to address a whirlwind of rumors surrounding Skilling's resignation. Sherron Watkins, a vice president who worked for Fastow, submitted an anonymous one-page letter that highlighted some of Fastow's SPE accounting manipulations for Lay to comment on at the all-employee meeting. Lay chose not to address Watkins' letter.

Watkins then claimed authorship of the letter, shared it with Enron's in-house lawyers, and scheduled a meeting with Lay for the following week to discuss the matter. The in-house lawyers strongly recommended that Watkins cancel her meeting with Lay until after Enron's chief legal counsel investigated her accusations about Fastow. After all, transactions between LJM and Enron had been approved by external auditors, external lawyers, and the Board of Directors.

DECISION CHOICE. If you were an Enron vice president, would you:

❶ Cancel your meeting with Lay and wait until hearing back from Enron's in-house lawyers?

❷ Continue your own investigation and meet with Lay at the already scheduled time?

(Continued)

In the Real World (continued)

❸ Confidentially notify Arthur Andersen about your suspicions?

❹ Confidentially notify the SEC about your suspicions?

❺ Confidentially notify *Wall Street Journal* reporters about your suspicions?

Why?

Effective Teams

Every work unit is a team. Go-getters, fence-sitters, and adversarial employees must learn how to operate as an effective team.

The foundation of effective team performance is trust.[4] Achieving highly desired collective results depends on employees being held accountable for them, which depends on employees being committed to the goal, which depends on constructive conflict, which depends on trust to speak openly. Trust is a core value for creating organizations of high integrity and superior performance.

Trust-building begins with the work unit's manager. Be open to other people's ideas and constructive criticism. Employees need to be free to ask for help or admit shortcomings and deficiencies without it being held against them.

Exhibit 10.2 provides a team effectiveness model.

Systematic Team Problem-Solving Process

Many work problems can be solved effectively and efficiently by a well-coached team of subordinates. Team members should develop

EXHIBIT 10.2

Team Effectiveness Model

Dysfunction	Positive Embodiment
1. Absence of Trust	Members of great teams trust one another on a fundamental, emotional level, and they are comfortable being vulnerable with each other about their weaknesses, mistakes, fears, and behaviors. They get to a point where they can be completely open with one another, without filters.
2. Fear of Conflict	Teams that trust one another are not afraid to engage in passionate dialogue around issues and decisions that are key to the organization's success. They do not hesitate to disagree with, challenge, and question one another, all in the spirit of finding the best answers, discovering the truth, and making great decisions.
3. Lack of Commitment	Teams that engage in unfiltered conflict are able to achieve genuine buy-in around important decisions, even when various members of the team initially disagree. That's because they ensure that all opinions and ideas are put on the table and considered, giving confidence to team members that no stone has been left unturned.
4. Avoidance of Accountability	Teams that commit to decisions and standards of performance do not hesitate to hold one another accountable for adhering to those decisions and standards. What is more, they don't rely on the team leader as the primary source of accountability, they go directly to their peers.

(Continued)

EXHIBIT 10.2	

(Continued)

Dysfunction	Positive Embodiment
5. Inattention to Collective Results	Teams that trust one another, engage in conflict, commit to decisions, and hold one another accountable are very likely to set aside their individual needs and agendas and focus almost exclusively on what is best for the team. They do not give in to the temptation to place their departments, career aspirations, or ego-driven status ahead of the collective results that define team success.

Patrick Lencioni, *Overcoming the Five Dysfunctions of a Team* (San Francisco: Jossey-Bass): 7; copyright 2001, with permission to adapt from John Wiley & Sons.

solutions to problems as they arise and, within reason, make the necessary changes.

Team problem solving requires training in two areas:

1. How to think through a problem

2. How to obtain relevant ideas from all team members

The scientific method of inquiry provides individuals and teams with a systematic five-stage process for thinking through a problem:

Stage 1: Define the problem

Stage 2: Identify alternative solutions

Stage 3: Evaluate and choose an alternative

Stage 4: Implement the decision

Stage 5: Monitor and control decision outcomes

If the outcome is unsatisfactory, then the problem under consideration might have to be defined differently, a different alternative solution pursued, or the change implementation better managed.

Managers must also systematically address the second issue—how to obtain relevant ideas from all team members. Employees have diverse personalities (see Chapter 7). Some people are introverted; others are extroverted. Extroverts are very willing to publicly share their ideas, while introverts are reticent to speak and tend to be more sensitive to criticism. If not appropriately managed, team discussions will be dominated by the viewpoints of extroverts.

The team problem-solving process below helps access each member's unique knowledge—introverts as well as extroverts—and generate solutions with the highest likelihood of achieving superior performance.

Step 1: Present the problem. Present the problem to all team members and address clarifying questions so all key issues are understood.

Step 2: Define individual solutions. Each team member individually writes down possible solutions to the problem.

Step 3: Present individual solutions. Each team member reads his or her solution to the entire team and the list of potential solutions recorded. Team members listen carefully without responding.

Step 4: Clarify individual solutions. Each team member explains his or her solution in greater detail and responds to clarifying questions. The solutions are not judged as good or bad.

Criticizing solutions during this step will inhibit introverted people from further participation.

Step 5: Brainstorm. For three minutes, team members should spontaneously propose as many solutions as possible, no matter how odd or impractical they might initially seem. New ideas can amend solutions already mentioned. Do not critique these new solutions yet. This step is likely to be dominated by extroverts. Make sure that introverted people are given an opportunity to express their new ideas.

Step 6: Group and prioritize solutions. As a team, organize the list of potential solutions according to common themes and prioritize them according to the greatest likelihood of success. Consider ease of implementation and costs when prioritizing the solutions. Develop action plans for implementing the best solutions.

Step 7: Play devil's advocate. Assign one team member the role of devil's advocate. This person should state all the reasons why the highest priority solution is likely to fail. Other team members should respond to these concerns and develop plans on how these obstacles and shortcomings could be managed.

Step 8: Implement and monitor. Have teams implement high-priority solutions that fall within the boundaries of their authority, and monitor the outcomes. Team members should present complex and costly solutions, or solutions that impact the operations of other work units, to the appropriate manager for further analysis.

Connecting Employees to the Mission— Appreciative Inquiry

Appreciative Inquiry is a team-based management technique that focuses on employee and organizational strengths.[5] Employees identify organizational processes that work well (*discover*), envision processes that would work well in the future (*dream*), plan and prioritize processes that would work well (*design*), and implement the proposals (*destiny*).

A key task of ethical leadership is aligning employee strengths so that employee weaknesses are irrelevant. Appreciative Inquiry is a particularly powerful method for aligning fence-sitters and adversarial employees, as well as go-getters, with continuous improvement efforts and superior performance.

The heart of an organization's mission is to serve customers. An Appreciative Inquiry workshop on superior customer service can be designed around the following steps:

Step 1: Individually reflect on superior customer service. Each employee independently responds to the following prompts:

- Describe a situation when *you received* superior customer service.

- Describe a situation when *you provided* superior customer service.

- Describe a situation when *a coworker provided* superior customer service.

- Describe other ways *the organization has provided* superior customer service.

- Describe other ways *the organization can provide* superior customer service.

- What *changes* would have to be made in the organization to achieve this?

Step 2: On a small team, determine the essential elements of superior customer service. Each team member presents situations when he or she received superior customer service, provided superior customer service, and observed others in the organization providing superior customer service. As a team, list the important elements mentioned in these stories that enabled employees to achieve superior customer service (e.g., "The common themes in these stories are x and y."). Share these elements with the larger group.

Step 3: Develop a collective vision of what is needed to achieve superior customer service. Each team member describes other ways the organization can provide superior customer service and changes that would have to be made to accomplish this. For instance, "We could provide superior customer service if we did x and y." As a team, develop a compelling image of how the organization can achieve superior customer service in the future. Share this image with the larger group.

Step 4: Create a draft of a new organizational mission statement that emphasizes superior customer service at every level of operations. Each team member independently composes a one-sentence mission statement and presents it to the team. As a team, achieve consensus on a one-sentence mission statement that meets the following four criteria, and share the mission statement with the larger group:

1. Is it desired? Would you want it?

2. Is it stated in affirmative and bold terms?

3. Is it clear and achievable?

4. Does it stretch and challenge the organization in a desired direction?

Step 5: Determine the organization's current "positive core." Each team member independently determines two or three core aspects of the organization that already support superior customer service. For each aspect, provide an example. For instance, "We are already good at doing x and y." As a team, reach consensus on the core aspects. Share the core aspects, and examples, with the larger group.

Step 6: Make personal commitments. Each team member independently lists what he or she will do more of, or differently, to deliver superior customer service. For instance, "I promise to do x, and y." Share this information with team members and hold each other accountable. Share these commitments with the larger group.

Step 7: Make organizational action recommendations. Each team member recommends initiatives for how the organization can achieve superior customer service. How can the vision and image (Step 3), mission statement (Step 4), current strengths (Step 5), and personal commitments (Step 6) become a highly integrated reality? As a team, further develop these recommendations and share with the larger group.

Step 8: Have management follow up. As an example of superior customer service and accountability, managers commit to providing feedback on this information within a reasonable timeframe.

Daily Performance Reflections

Members of an empowered team not only address problems as they arise and participate in long-term planning, but also share their daily accomplishments and lessons learned with other team members.

Set aside 10 to 15 minutes at the end of every day for teams to process the events that occurred during the day and make preparations for managing any ongoing problems the following day. Organize daily reflections where employees share the following information about the work day:

- A performance accomplishment or satisfaction experienced
- A problem that arose
- How the problem was solved
- A lesson learned from the accomplishment or problem that might benefit other team members
- A problem that still needs to be addressed

Begin the daily performance reflections with a success story, and make others aware how each employee made a difference in organizational operations. Discussing how a problem was solved deepens employee empowerment. Concluding the meeting by discussing ongoing problems provides other team members an opportunity to share potential solutions and establishes hope that the situation will be resolved soon.

Scanlon-Type Gainsharing Plans

Scanlon-type gainsharing plans provide nonmanagement employees with institutional responsibility and accountability for improving operations.[6] Work unit teams elicit, evaluate, and implement continuous improvement suggestions, and receive financial rewards for surpassing historical performance standards. Gainsharing has been successfully implemented in many types of organizations, including factories, hospitals, restaurants, and government offices.

Five elements of a Scanlon-type gainsharing plan are:

1. *Suggestion system.* Employees submit written suggestions to the gainsharing coordinator on how to improve efficiency, reduce costs, and increase revenue. The suggestions are listed in a log book and sent to the appropriate work team.

2. *Gainsharing team.* A gainsharing team consists of either all nonmanagement employees in the work unit or representatives voted to the team. The teams can be defined in terms of job tasks (all nurses) or location (everyone on the third floor of a hospital). Teams meet weekly or monthly to review suggestions and brainstorm solutions. The teams have a monthly budget to implement suggestions that fall within their domain. Suggestions that exceed the team's monthly budget, or that impact other work units, are forwarded to a review board.

3. *Review board.* The review board consists of one representative from each gainsharing team, the gainsharing coordinator, and relevant managers. The nonmanagement representatives report on the changes their teams implemented and respond to questions. They also present suggestions that exceed their monthly budget allocations or impact other work units. Review board members reach a consensus on whether to implement these more costly or inter–work unit suggestions.

4. *Gainsharing coordinator.* The gainsharing coordinator is responsible for managing the gainsharing system. The coordinator is typically a go-getter nonmanagement employee or human resources manager, and the duties include managing the suggestion system process, training team members, attending team meetings, and maintaining records. This can be a full-time position or added to an employee's current job duties.

5. *Group-based financial bonus.* A group-based financial bonus calculation is devised that compares projected costs and actual costs for a given period of time, usually a month. The projected costs are based on historical performance, usually an average of the previous three years. The cost calculation can be very broad (e.g., the total value of goods and services divided by labor costs) or narrow (e.g., electricity costs divided by labor costs). When actual costs are lower than the projected historical cost, the financial difference is shared between the employees and organization, typically on a 50/50 ratio.

Half of the nonmanagement employees' share is then distributed as a bonus. The other half is set aside in a year-end reserve pool that accounts for months where actual costs exceed projected historical costs. Any amount remaining in the reserve pool at the end of the year is then distributed among the nonmanagement employees.

Open Book Management

Transparency is an essential element of trust-building. Open Book Management is a technique where managers share relevant financial and operational information with nonmanagement employees so they can make better informed decisions.[7] The information shared could include balance sheets, revenue, profit, cost of goods, customer returns, on-time shipments, and so on.

Trusting nonmanagement employees with previously confidential financial and operational information enables them to behave more like managers. More than 3,000 companies use some form of Open Book Management, including units at Allstate Insurance, Sprint, and Amoco.[8]

TIPS AND TECHNIQUES

Open Book Management

To optimize Open Book Management success, provide employees with:

1 Relevant financial and operational information for decision-making purposes.

2 Training to understand the numbers critical for tracking organizational performance.

3 Training to understand how their daily activities impact the financial and operational targets.

(Continued)

Determine which data are critical for the employees to know. Meet with teams to jointly establish challenging goals aligned with organizational goals (see Chapter 9). Display scoreboards in public areas that measure progress toward targeted goals. The bonus reinforces the idea that employees are valuable partners in improving performance. Greater access to planning and budgeting information enables employees to foresee the need for change.

Profit Sharing

Providing employees with a share of company profits is also very ethical, motivating, and empowering. These financial reward plans supplement, but do not replace, base pay. When the company does well, the employees financially benefit. As a result, employees feel empowered to work as if they are owners. Researchers report that profit sharing has positive impacts on employee cooperation, turnover, productivity, costs, and profits.[9]

Profit-sharing companies set aside a percentage of profits beyond a targeted amount in a bonus pool. Some companies distribute profits as a percentage of compensation, under the assumption that higher-paid employees contribute more to the financial outcome. Other companies create a multifactor calculation that allows for bonus fluctuations based on team and individual accomplishments.

Profits are distributed in cash or stock at the end of the fiscal year, or as deferred compensation. The deferred compensation is not taxed until accessed by the employee, usually upon retirement, death, disability, or employment termination. Employees can borrow money against their profit-sharing account.

Profit-sharing plans are governed by the Employee Retirement Security Act (ERISA). Employer contributions cannot exceed an average of 15% of an employee's salary during any two-year period. Employers can deduct profit sharing as a business expense.

The profit-sharing plan can enhance organizational loyalty by spreading out the length of time required for an employee to have full access to the funds. Typically, an employee is fully vested after three to six years. If an employee leaves the organization prior to being fully vested, the amount remaining in the employee's profit sharing account is redistributed to the other plan participants.

Stock Options

Stock options, historically reserved for executives, are now offered by many public and private companies to all employees.[10] More than 10,000 Microsoft employees have become millionaires through its stock option plan.

Stock options give an employee the right to purchase a specific number of company shares at a fixed price by a particular future date, typically 10 years. The number of stock options an employee receives is based on a formula, usually determined by percentage of compensation to total payroll and performance accomplishments. Design stock option plans to reward, and retain, the go-getters. Employees often have full vesting rights after three to five years, and are taxed on the profits earned when they option to buy and sell their stock.

An *employee stock purchase plan* is slightly different. Employees can have deductions taken out of their pay and put into an account to purchase stock at a discount, usually 15%, by a specified date. Some companies will match a certain percentage of the employee deduction. If the employee decides not to purchase the company's stock by the expiration date, the employee gets his or her pay deductions back.

Some privately-held companies, whose stocks are not sold on the open market, offer employees *phantom stock*. The phantom stock value of privately owned companies is annually determined by an independent appraiser. Phantom stock can also be issued by publicly held companies that do not want to dilute the ownership rights of existing shareholders.

Similar to stock options, phantom stock has a specified expiration date and can be structured in different ways. Many companies use the phantom stock as a bonus system, in which an employee earns a cash bonus equal to the increase in the phantom stock's value between the day issued and the day exercised.

Employee Stock Option Plans (ESOPs)

Employee stock option plans (ESOPs), established in 1957, take stock options one step further in empowering employees. The company gives all full-time employees over the age of 21 a significant equity stake in the company.[11]

Typically, the owner borrows money to purchase company stock and places the shares in a trust fund. The loan interest is tax deductible and paid off through dividends. Loan principal payments are deductible up to 25% of payroll.

The stocks are then allocated into employee accounts according to a specific formula. The company makes annual tax-deductible contributions into the fund to purchase stock employees sell back to the company. Most of the money in the trust fund must be invested primarily in the company. The value of employee stock is independently appraised on an annual basis. The value of the stock increase is tax deferred until sold.

Employees can purchase their vested shares when they leave the organization—quit, are fired, die, or retire—and must sell the stock back to the company or other employees within one year at the appraised value.

Employees can vote their ESOP shares on major issues. ESOPs are governed by a board of directors that employs professional managers. In publicly held companies, ESOP participants have the same rights as other stockholders.

Cooperatives

Producer, consumer, and employee cooperatives are an alternative way to raise capital and govern a business. In a *producer* cooperative, such as an agricultural cooperative, producers pool their capital and resources for their mutual benefit. Similarly, *consumer* cooperatives are businesses owned by customers for their mutual benefit, such as credit unions and healthcare cooperatives. In both circumstances, profits are either reinvested in the cooperative or distributed among the owners (producers or consumers).

Employee cooperatives are organizations owned by the employees and democratically governed—one vote per employee-owner. Employee cooperatives can be found in a wide range of industries and organizations, including agriculture, banks, food stores, coffee, home health care, technology, and poultry.[12]

Each employee-owned cooperative creates its own unique rules. In some cooperatives, the employee-owners vote on board members, managers, capital investments, wages, and company policies. Large cooperatives tend to elect a board of directors that determines major strategic issues and hires managers. Profits are reinvested in the organization, set aside in reserves, or distributed to the employee-owners based on an agreed-upon formula.

Equal Exchange, founded in 1986, is one of the largest employee cooperatives in the United States.[13] All employees have the right to vote (one vote per employee, not per share), right to serve as a manager or board director, right to information (Open Book Management), and right to freedom of speech within the organization. Of Equal Exchange's net profits, 7% is donated to nonprofit organizations and 3% is invested in other employee cooperatives. Two-thirds of the remaining 90 percent net profit is reinvested in the organization, and one-third is divided equally among the employee-owners.

Summary

Organizations of superior performance place a high value on trust and responsibility. Trust increases when employees are treated like managers or owners and the barriers between management and nonmanagement employees have been minimized.

This chapter explored a wide variety of management systems and techniques for involving employees in the organization's decision-making process and providing financial rewards for improved organizational performance. In an empowered organization, employees not only make and implement decisions on a daily basis that improve organizational operations, but also share in the profits that they helped to create.

Notes

1. Richard D. White, "Organizational Design and Ethics: The Effects of Rigid Hierarchy on Moral Reasoning," *International Journal of Organization Theory & Behavior*, 2, nos. 3 and 4 (1999): 431–456.

2. Denis Collins, *Gainsharing and Power: Lessons from Six Scanlon Plans* (Ithaca, NY: Cornell University Press, 1998).

3. Mark C. Bolino and William H. Turnley, "Going the Extra Mile: Cultivating and Managing Employee Citizenship Behavior," *Academy of Management Executive*, 17, no. 3 (2003): 60–71.

4. Patrick Lencioni, *Overcoming the Five Dysfunctions of a Team* (San Francisco: Jossey-Bass, 2005).

5. David L. Cooperrider and Diana Whitney, *Appreciative Inquiry: A Positive Revolution in Change* (San Francisco: Berrett-Koehler, 2005); see the Web site: http://appreciativeinquiry.case.edu/default.cfm, accessed 9/18/08.

6. Denis Collins, *Gainsharing and Power: Lessons from Six Scanlon Plans* (Ithaca, NY: Cornell University Press, 1998).

7. John Case, *Open-Book Management: The Coming Business Revolution* (New York: Collins Business, 1996).

8. John Case, *The Open-Book Experience: Lessons from Over 100 Companies Who Successfully Transformed Themselves* (New York: Basic Books, 1998).

9. Raymond A. Noe, John R. Hollenbeck, Barry Gerhart, and Patrick M. Wright, *Human Resources Management*, 5th edition (New York: McGraw-Hill Irwin, 2006).

10. "A Comprehensive Overview of Employee Ownership," National Center for Employee Ownership, www.nceo.org, accessed 9/18/08.

11. Joseph Blasi, Douglas Kruse, and Aaron Bernstein, *In the Company of Owners: The Truth about Stock Options* (New York, NY: Basic Books, 2003); also, see www.nceo.org, "A Comprehensive Overview of Employee Ownership," National Center for Employee Ownership, at www.nceo.org, accessed 9/18/08.

12. Frank Adams and Gary Hansen, *Putting Democracy to Work: A Practical Guide for Starting and Managing Worker-Owned Businesses* (San Francisco: Berrett-Koehler Publishers, 1993); see also www.usworker.coop, accessed 9/18/08.

13. www.equalexchange.com/worker-owned, accessed 9/18/08.

PART 4

Being a Good Citizen

CHAPTER 11

Environmental Management

After reading this chapter, you will be able to:

- Articulate the competitive advantages of being eco-friendly
- Manage the environmental change process
- Create an Environmental Management System plan
- Identify environmental risks
- Develop measureable environmental goals and objectives
- Assess environmental performance

Treating the Earth with respect is one of the greatest ethical management challenges. For centuries, managers have treated the 4.5 billion year old Earth as an unlimited resource to be exploited. Business response to environmental problems has evolved from denial, up until the 1960s, to eco-efficiency and sustainable management in the 2000s.

A growing number of managers now realize that appropriately managing the relationship between organizational operations and the environment can enhance profits and long-term success, as well as quality of life for current and future generations.

This chapter explores how superior environmental performance can be achieved by integrating environmental impacts with an organization's decision-making process and performance assessments. Environmental management is a competitive advantage that saves the organization money, enhances its reputation, and attracts and motivates employees.

Competitive Advantages of Being Eco-Friendly

An increasing number of organizations are being recognized for "going green." The media is particularly fond of highlighting the accomplishments of green companies. Many magazine, television, and radio Web sites provide Internet links to environmental exemplars, which results in free publicity. Environmental advocacy groups also direct consumers to green products and businesses. Green shopping Web sites make it easy for consumers to use eco-friendliness as a purchasing criterion.[1] Co-op America's online *National Green Pages* sorts more than 10,000 eco-friendly products for consumer searches.[2]

Similar to the marketing of ethics and diversity programs within an organization, managers should emphasize the business case when communicating the need for superior environmental performance. Exhibit 11.1 summarizes some of the many economic and organizational benefits of being eco-friendly.

EXHIBIT 11.1

Benefits of Being Eco–Friendly

Issue	Explanation
Production cost savings	Eco-efficiency reduces energy and material costs of production.
Lower insurance premiums	Insurance companies are including sustainable development initiatives in the underwriting process.
Lower bank loan rates	Major banks conduct environmental risk analysis as part of lending money for mortgage and land acquisitions.
Reduced liability risks	Federal and state governments hold polluters responsible for cleanup costs, property damages, and other related costs.
Market expansion	One of the fastest growth markets is for new "green" technologies and products.
Customer attraction and retention	Customers are demanding higher environmental standards when making product decisions.
Employee recruitment	Young professionals strongly consider eco-friendliness when evaluating job opportunities.
Higher employee commitment	Environmental reputation enhances employee morale, commitment, and effort.
Reduced product design to market time	Failure to anticipate new environmental regulations delays new product introductions.
Regulatory flexibility	Organizations with an environmental management system (EMS) may be granted greater regulatory flexibility.
Industry self-regulation	Enhances trust and practical, cost-effective self-regulatory legislation.

(Continued)

EXHIBIT 11.1

(Continued)

Issue	Explanation
Socially responsible mutual funds	Inclusion in the increasing number of CSR fund screens affects share price.
Better relations with community	Increases community acceptance of new project startups and expansions.
Better activist and media relations	Negative activist attention creates long-term public relations problems.
Personal integrity	Personal commitment to good stewardship generates pride.

Brian Nattrass and Mary Altomare, *The Natural Step for Business: Wealth, Ecology and the Evolutionary Corporation* (British Columbia, Canada: New Society Publishers): 193; copyright 1999, with permission to adapt from New Society Publishers.

Determine which of these competitive advantages are most meaningful for improving organizational performance and use the reasons to justify, and support, environmental management initiatives. Managers, by the nature of their job responsibilities, have many tasks to perform within a limited amount of time. A bottom-line approach to environmental management change increases the likelihood of managers valuing it more heavily.

Wal-Mart is an organization that understands the link between eco-friendliness and profits. Wal-Mart is the nation's largest private user of electricity and owns the second-largest fleet of trucks. In 2005, the company's short-term sustainability goals included 25% efficiency increases in fleet vehicles, a 30% reduction in store energy use, and a 25% reduction in solid waste.

These reductions have generated tremendous savings and revenue opportunities for Wal-Mart. Eliminating excessive packaging on its private-label line of toys saved $2.4 million in annual shipping costs; installing auxiliary power units on trucks saved $26 million annually in fuel costs; and installing balers to recycle and sell plastics generated $28 million in extra revenue.

Managing the Environmental Change Process

Becoming an eco-friendly organization requires leadership from the CEO or President. Primary responsibility for implementation, however, should be assigned to one particular manager. Depending on company size, the environmental champion could be the Environmental Health & Safety Director, an environmental manager, or a manager whose multiple duties include environmental performance.

Greening the organization is a concept that is well-regarded by employees and relatively easy for them to rally behind. According to a Society for Human Resource Management survey, three-quarters of the employees in companies without an environmental program want to "go green."[3]

Some green organizations create an "environmental mission statement" that clearly articulates the organization's relationship with the natural environment. Similar to a Code of Ethics, the environmental mission statement should be used as a foundation for determining and assessing organizational actions.

The Starbucks environmental mission statement in Exhibit 11.2 begins with the need to integrate concern for the environment in all aspects of operations and highlights the interrelationship between profits and environmental performance.[4]

EXHIBIT 11.2

Starbucks Environmental Mission Statement

Starbucks is committed to a role of environmental leadership in all facets of our business.

We will fulfill this mission by a commitment to:

Understanding environmental issues and sharing information with our partners.

Developing innovative and flexible solutions to bring about change.

Striving to buy, sell and use environmentally friendly products.

Recognizing that fiscal responsibility is essential to our environmental future.

Instilling environmental responsibility as a corporate value.

Measuring and monitoring our progress for each project.

Encouraging all partners to share in our mission.

Environmental activities cut across departments and work units. Managers should create a cross-functional Green Committee composed of go-getters to address common concerns, share knowledge, and ensure successful implementation of action plans. Committee duties can include acknowledging previous environmental accomplishments, gathering relevant data, engaging employees in small incremental changes, addressing interdepartmental issues, inspiring employees by taking on a large project that has a high likelihood of success, enhancing customer and supplier awareness of environmental efforts, and communicating environmental successes to other employees.

Exhibit 11.3 summarizes ten aspects of the environmental change process, beginning with the importance of an environmental manager accountable for initiatives.

EXHIBIT 11.3

Managing Environmental Change

Aspect	Focus/Objectives	Tools and Methodologies
Environmental Manager	One manager is accountable for environmental initiatives.	The environmental manager is a leadership position requiring political skills and broad knowledge of organizational operations.
Top Management Support	Obtain vocal and visible support from CEO, COO, and other executives.	Ask CEO and others about their environmental vision for the firm; introduce top management to the business case for sustainability; request that they convey this message to rest of the organization.
Green Committee	Achieve buy-in from work units throughout the organization.	Choose go-getters from different work units to oversee environmental performance, elicit ideas, and manage the implementation of action plans.
Vision and Strategy	Develop the vision of a sustainable firm in a sustainable society.	Integrate eco-friendliness into vision, strategy, and financial models; link environmental action plans to the vision and strategy.

(Continued)

EXHIBIT 11.3

(Continued)

Aspect	Focus/Objectives	Tools and Methodologies
Training, Education, Coaching	Use coaching style to educate all employees about putting environmental principles into practice.	Adapt training materials to specific organizational context and employee work units; train the trainers and coaches; develop engaging training materials.
Employee Involvement	Team-building activities, encourage suggestions, continual reinforcement.	Teams focus on reducing wastes and resources used; follow-through on employee suggestions; friendly competition among employees and work units.
Practical Application and Innovation	Identify "low-hanging fruit," practical ideas for change.	Develop mechanisms for reviewing suggestions and innovations; provide resources to experiment and try new ideas; ongoing coaching; share lessons learned.
Feedback and Measurement	Benchmark, track, measure, evaluate, provide feedback, and reward results.	Develop baseline measures, document, and post results; translate resource savings into financial language; recognize and communicate achievements.
Influence	Employees, suppliers, customers, competitors, shareholders, community.	Encourage all stakeholders to attend workshops; partner with other groups; educate suppliers and customers through booklets, product labels, annual reports, and Web site resources.

| Integrate into all Business Functions | Make sustainability a normal business consideration. | Implement an environmental management system (EMS); address at all meetings and include in all reports; include in business plan, performance evaluations, and bonuses. |

Brian Nattrass and Mary Altomare, *The Natural Step for Business: Wealth, Ecology and the Evolutionary Corporation* (British Columbia, Canada: 'New Society Publishers): 152–153; copyright 1999, with permission to adapt from New Society Publishers.

Environmental Management System (EMS)

The International Organization for Standardization (ISO), a non-governmental organization, has worked closely with industry, technical experts, and other stakeholders to develop an environmental management system (EMS) plan for achieving superior environmental performance.[5] Organizations can be certified for meeting ISO standards. ISO certification is a source of company pride and a competitive advantage in a marketplace where more organizations and consumers are using a green screen to choose suppliers.

The EMS plan is a document that describes how the organization conducts environmental policy development, environmental planning, environmental implementation, environmental monitoring and corrective actions, and management review. The document must contain sufficient detail for an employee to understand how these environmental processes operate.

Exhibit 11.4 highlights procedures to document for each of the five EMS sections. An employee, after reviewing the EMS, should know exactly what to do if she or he wants to propose a new environmental policy or make an environmental performance recommendation.

EXHIBIT 11.4

An Environmental Management System (EMS) Outline

What are the procedures for:

Environmental Policy

- Developing environmental policies?

Environmental Planning

- Identifying operations that impact the environment?
- Identifying environmental risks?
- Identifying applicable environmental laws and regulations?
- Establishing short- and long-term environmental objectives and targets?
- Developing action plans aimed at achieving the environmental objectives and targets?

Environmental Implementation and Operation

- Determining who is responsible for specific aspects of environmental performance?
- Determining and developing environmental training activities?
- Developing environmental emergency plans?
- Communicating environmental issues and accomplishments to employees and external stakeholders?

Environmental Checking and Corrective Action

- Maintaining records related to environmental performance?
- Monitoring and assessing key environmental objectives and performance measures?

- Determining corrective actions?
- Auditing the EMS?

Management Review

- Managerial review of environmental performance, including responses to environmental emergencies and the adequacy of environmental accomplishments?

Annually audit the EMS to ensure that the procedures are operating effectively.

Environmental Risk Assessment

A key aspect of an EMS is managing environmental risk. Each organization has a unique set of environmental input, throughput, and output risks. The environmental risk assessment should consider the environmental performance of suppliers, because they can significantly disrupt organizational operations. Sony incurred very negative publicity when illegal cadmium was found in PlayStation cables purchased from suppliers.[6]

Exhibit 11.5 provides a list of questions to consider when performing an environmental risk assessment. Answering these questions can help organizations identify environmental risks within the supplier–operations–customer value chain.[7]

The environmental risk assessment in Exhibit 11.5 is, as much as possible, based on objective information. Calculating risk is an art, not a science, and requires impartiality and rationality. Managers, however, tend to make risk assumptions that are biased toward a

EXHIBIT 11.5

Identifying Environmental Risks

Value Chain Phase	Sample Questions to Help Identify Environmental Risk
Suppliers	• What substances go into the products suppliers sell to us? Are they toxic? • What resources (energy, water, and materials) are our suppliers most dependent on? Are they abundant or constrained, now and in the near future? • Do our suppliers pollute? Do they meet all applicable laws? Will legal requirements get tighter for them?
Company Operations	• How big is our environmental footprint? • What resources are we most dependent on and how much do we use? • What emissions do we release into the air or water? • How do we dispose of waste? • How up to date is our environmental management system? • What are the chances of a spill, leak, or release of hazardous materials? • Have others in our industry had problems? • What local, state, federal, or international regulations apply to our business? Are we in full compliance? Are these regulations getting tighter?
Customers	• Are there hazardous substances in our products? • How much energy (or water or other resources) does our product require customers to use? • What do customers do with our products when they are done with them? • What would happen if we are required to take the products back?

Daniel C. Esty and Andrew S. Winston, *Green to Gold* (New Haven, CT: Yale University Press): 117; copyright 2006, with permission to adapt from Yale University Press.

favored outcome. Enron's executive team, for instance, made several assumptions about how the stock market would respond to the amount of losses Ken Lay could announce in October 2001 (see *In the Real World: Announcing Third-Quarter Results—October 2001*). They assigned the least amount of risk to the strategy that would cause them the least amount of public embarrassment (minimal disclosure), a risk assessment bias that would contribute to Enron's implosion.

IN THE REAL WORLD

Announcing Third-Quarter Results—October 2001

Sherron Watkins, refusing to be bullied by corporate lawyers, met with Ken Lay in late August to discuss Fastow's accounting manipulations. Lay did not seem to fully grasp the depth of the accounting problems Watkins described, though he promised to look more deeply into the matter. Watkins also informed a contact at Arthur Andersen, who then sent a memo summarizing his conversation with Watkins to David Duncan, Andersen's lead auditor on the Enron account.

In late August 2001, Enron's Chief Accounting Officer Richard Causey informed Lay that he and Fastow, with Skilling's knowledge, had hidden losses totaling nearly $7 billion the past few years. As CEO, Lay was responsible for these numbers, but he simply hadn't been paying close attention. Lay had always let others he trusted, such as Skilling, Causey, and Fastow, manage the details while he lobbied politicians and potential customers around the world.

(Continued)

On September 11, 2001, shortly after Lay found out about the hidden losses, terrorists hijacked two airplanes and crashed them into the World Trade Center towers, brutally killing more than 3,000 innocent people. When the stock market reopened, many stocks nosedived, including Enron's.

Causey was responsible for preparing Enron's third-quarter financial statements, scheduled for release on October 16. Lay now faced a decision that would directly impact 20,000 Enron employees—how honest should he be with investors about Enron's hidden losses? CEOs have a fiduciary duty to honestly convey financial information to shareholders. But Enron's accounting books were a mess, and nobody was absolutely sure as to the exact amount of financial losses Enron had sustained the past few years.

Wall Street analysts predicted that Enron had third-quarter losses totaling $2 billion due to the nationwide recession, Internet business collapse, and terrorist attack.

Lay met with several trusted Enron executives to brainstorm his options. They recommended that Lay report only $1.2 billion of the estimated $7 billion in losses, because that amount could be reasonably explained without damaging Enron's already falling stock price too much. In addition, beating Wall Street expectations might attract new investors.

The executives also pointed out that if Lay reported all $7 billion in losses on October 16, Enron's stock price would collapse from a massive stock sell off, causing Enron to default on its loans. A resultant government investigation could quickly bankrupt the company. Many Enron employees, who had loaded their pension funds with Enron's soaring stock the last few years despite being told to diversify, would lose their entire life savings.

DECISION CHOICE. If you were the CEO of Enron, how much of the hidden losses would you report to the public when announcing third quarter results on October 16:

❶ All $7 billion in losses, and risk financial collapse?

❷ $2 billion in losses, to match Wall Street expectations?

❸ $1.2 billion in losses, as recommended by some Enron executives?

Why?

The Natural Step (TNS) Framework and Cost Reductions

An increasing number of communities and businesses are using The Natural Step (TNS) framework as a conceptual tool for environmental analysis and action plan development.[8] The TNS framework attributes the root causes of environmental problems to four issues: removing too many substances from the Earth's crust, producing too many synthetic compounds that are difficult for nature to break down, manipulating the ecosystem, and inefficiently and unfairly meeting human needs worldwide.

The TNS framework is a very good beginning point for determining what changes in organizational operations could improve environmental performance. The following three TNS objectives should be explored by work units, total quality management teams, or gainsharing teams. The three objectives are aimed at reducing the use of resources that damage environmental well-being.

Objective #1—Reduce Wasteful Dependence on Fossil Fuels and Underground Metals and Minerals

- What scarce minerals and materials does the organization use?

- How can the scarce minerals and materials be substituted with minerals and materials that are more abundant in nature?

- How can the organization use its mined materials more efficiently?

Objective #2—Reduce Wasteful Dependence on Chemicals and Synthetic Compounds

- What chemicals and synthetic compounds does the organization use?

- How can the chemicals and synthetic compounds be substituted with natural compounds or those that break down more easily in nature?

- How can the organization use its synthetic compounds more efficiently?

Objective #3—Reduce Encroachment on Nature

- What land, water, and wildlife resources does the organization use?

- Are any of the organization's uses of land, water, and wildlife resources unnecessary?

- How can the organization use its land, water, and wildlife resources more efficiently?

After applying the TNS analysis, create a list of issues the organization could address to improve its environmental performance. Use the eight-step team problem-solving process described in Chapter 10 to develop and prioritize solutions. Then pick a "low-hanging fruit"—an inexpensive solution that is relatively easy to implement. Closely monitor the potential obstacles raised by the devil's advocate. Success in achieving the low-hanging fruit solution will help employees gain the confidence needed to successfully implement more complicated solutions.

Cost reduction areas most organizations focus on, and what can be done about them, include:

- *Energy reduction*—Ask the local public utility to perform an energy audit and provide onsite consultation.

- *Waste disposal reduction*—Document organizational waste within each work unit. Determine how to eliminate it or locate organizations willing to purchase or use the waste.

- *Paper reduction*—Conduct communications through e-mail, rather than using paper, and develop an online document storage system.

- *Product shipment reduction*—Examine how suppliers transport products to the organization and how the organization transports products to its customers. Determine alternative methods to more effectively receive and disburse these deliveries, including less packaging material.

- *Toxic substances reduction*—Develop a list of toxic substances used at the workplace. The number of suppliers providing nontoxic alternatives is a growing market. These products can reduce product disposal costs and positively impact employee health.

- *Business travel reduction*—Document the amount of business travel conducted during a particular time period. Determine which offsite meetings could have been conducted through teleconferencing, video-conferencing, or interactive e-mail communications.

Office Depot's Advice on How to Save Money By Going Green[9]

- Energy Star–qualified office equipment saves up to 75% in electricity use.

- Compact fluorescent bulbs last 10 times longer than incandescent bulbs and save electricity.

- Power strips save electricity.

- Daylighting saves electricity.

- Remanufactured ink and toner cartridges cost an average of 15% less than national brands and come with a 100% money back quality guarantee.

- Recycle empty ink and toner cartridges for discounted prices.

- Use digital storage solutions.

- Donate unwanted products and furniture for tax deductions.

- Use reusable coffee mugs instead of disposable cups.

The next two sections discuss product packaging and design and building design, both of which have potentially high cost savings.

Product Packaging and Design

The European Union's Packaging and Packaging Waste Directive, passed in 1994, provides a glimpse into a major environmental management trend that is likely to impact business operations in the United States.[10] Businesses are responsible for directly recovering and recycling product packaging or paying a Green Dot licensing fee to a third party that collects and recycles the packaging.

Packaging refers to both the package immediately surrounding the product and the transportation container—everything except the product itself. The law covers cardboard, plastic, metals, wood, paper, crates, drums, pallets, and Styrofoam containers.

Environmentalists anticipate legislating "cradle-to-cradle" laws that would regulate the product itself, in addition to its packaging. Products can be designed to achieve zero waste, which would mean no end to the product life cycle. After use, the product would be broken down into its component parts, which would then be reused or recycled, rather than disposed of in a landfill.

Green Buildings

The United States Green Building Council's Leadership in Energy and Environmental Design (LEED) rating system provides eco-friendly measurement standards for certifying building construction and remodeling.[11] Some organizations use LEED's building guidelines but do not apply for certification because of documentation cost issues or a lack of interest in being officially certified.

The four levels of LEED certification are: Basic (26 points), Silver (32 points), Gold (39 points), and Platinum (52 points). Exhibit 11.6 provides examples of eco-friendly practices, and the number of points available, for each of the six LEED innovation and design categories.[12] Mandatory practices for certification are noted with an asterisk. PowerPoint presentations about LEED certification are available on the United States Green Building Council Web site.[13]

EXHIBIT 11.6

The LEED Rating System

Category	Points	Examples of Best Practices
Sustainable Sites	14	• Erosion and sedimentation control* • Appropriateness of selected site • Urban redevelopment • Brownfield redevelopment • Alternative transportation availability • Stormwater runoff management
Water Efficiency	5	• Water-use efficiency for landscaping • Innovative wastewater technologies • Water-use efficiency within the building
Energy and Atmosphere	17	• Fundamental building systems verified by a commissioning agent* • Appropriate energy efficiency level established for the base building and systems* • Zero use of chlorofluorocarbon (CFC)–based refrigerants in HVAC&R systems* • Optimize energy performance • Renewable energy use
Materials and Resources	13	• Collection and storage of recyclables generated by building occupants* • Recycle or reuse construction waste • Use salvaged, refurbished, or reused materials for construction • Construction material used has recycled content • Local/regional building materials and products

| Indoor Environ-mental Quality | 15 | • Appropriate indoor air quality (IAQ) level established*
• Tobacco smoke control system*
• Carbon dioxide monitoring
• Ventilation effectiveness
• IAQ management plan
• Low-emitting VOC products
• Thermal comfort
• Occupied areas have daylight and outdoor views |
| Innovation and Design Process | 5 | • Innovation in design beyond LEED requirements
• LEED-accredited professional on building construction team |

*Indicates a required practice

Environmental Performance Indicators

Continuous environmental improvement entails creating historical benchmarks for previous environmental performance, measuring current environmental performance, and developing goals and targets for future environmental performance.

Each organization has a unique set of environmental impacts. The environmental planning section of an EMS, discussed earlier in this chapter, summarizes the organization's environmental impacts. The Natural Step section of this chapter suggests areas for environmental impact reductions. Next, managers should gather information to measure these impacts and document continuous improvement.

Climate Care provides a simple Internet-based carbon calculator for business use.[14] The calculator requires data for office carbon dioxide consumption, company travel mileage, freight mileage and weight,

EXHIBIT 11.7	
Key Environmental Metrics	
Category	**Basic Metrics**
Energy	• Energy used • Renewable energy used or bought
Water	• Total water used • Water pollution
Air	• Greenhouse gas emissions • Releases of heavy metals and toxic chemicals • Emissions of particulates, VOCs, SOx, and NOx
Waste	• Hazardous waste • Solid waste • Recycled materials
Transportation	• Company vehicle mileage • Business travel mileage • Freight mileage and tonnage
Compliance	• Notices of violations • Fines or penalties paid

Daniel C. Esty and Andrew S. Winston, *Green to Gold* (New Haven, CT: Yale University Press): 175; copyright 2006, with permission to adapt from Yale University Press.

and additional carbon emissions. Exhibit 11.7 offers a more extensive list of environmental measures relevant to most organizations.

Link environmental performance measures to organizational strategy. If an organization is in a growth strategy, for instance, an increase in energy use could be a very healthy sign. A more useful measure might be a ratio composed of energy use per revenue dollars.[15] Share the performance indicator results with all employees so they know whether improvement is occurring, and use the results as benchmarks for new goals and targets.

Some organizations obtain carbon neutrality by purchasing carbon offsets equivalent to their carbon footprint. Offset products include investing in tree plantings and forestry projects, clean and renewable energy projects, and energy efficiency projects in other parts of the world. Organizations can also purchase carbon credits from climate exchanges, which reduce the amount of carbon credits available to high-polluting organizations.

An environmental financial statement is another type of performance indicator. Baxter International's environmental financial statement quantifies the financial impact of its global environmental management program.[16] Baxter's environmental programs have generated $82.6 million in cost savings from 2002 through 2007, triple the cost of its environmental programs.

Sustainability Reporting

Global Reporting Initiative (GRI), an international multi-stakeholder coalition, provides general guidelines for sustainability reporting that allow for some environmental performance comparisons between organizations.[17] The guidelines have been used by more than 1,500 organizations, including large corporations, small businesses, NGOs, and public agencies.

The GRI reporting framework was developed with input from businesses, investors, accountants, and activists, and takes into account economic, environmental, and social performance measures.

The environmental performance section discusses EMS variables and provides performance measures for environmental inputs (e.g., material, energy, water) and outputs (e.g., emissions, effluents, waste). In 2006, after extensive public review and feedback, GRI released the third generation of reporting guidelines.

Summary

Ethical organizations place a high value on appropriately managing the Earth's scarce resources and creating environmentally healthy workplaces for their employees. Eco-friendly organizations tend to have lower energy costs and find it easier to attract and maintain high-quality employees.

This chapter explored a wide variety of environmental management techniques. Organizations can achieve superior environmental performance by:

- Managing the environmental change process
- Creating an EMS plan that documents relevant organizational procedures
- Conducting an environmental risk assessment
- Using TNS objectives to develop action plans
- Redesigning the product to achieve zero waste
- Operating in green buildings
- Developing performance indicators to measure continuous improvement
- Reporting the results of these efforts

Organizations adopting these procedures will reduce costs, be a step ahead of regulatory trends, and contribute to the environmental well-being of future generations.

Notes

1. www.greenchoices.org, accessed 9/23/08; www.naturalcollection.com, accessed 9/23/08; www.greenfibres.com, accessed 9/23/08.
2. www.coopamerica.org, accessed 9/23/08.
3. Society for Human Resource Management, "Green Workplace Survey," January 16, 2008, www.shrm.org/surveys, accessed 9/23/08.
4. www.starbucks.com/aboutus/environment.asp, accessed August 18, 2008.
5. www.iso.org/iso/home.htm, accessed 9/23/08.
6. Pete Engardio, "Beyond the Green Corporation," *Business Week*, January 29, 2007.
7. Daniel C. Esty and Andrew S. Winston, *Green to Gold* (New Haven, CT: Yale University Press, 2006): 117.
8. Brian Nattrass and Mary Altomare, *The Natural Step for Business: Wealth, Ecology and the Evolutionary Corporation* (British Columbia, Canada: New Society Publishers, 1999); see also www.naturalstep.org, accessed 9/23/08.
9. www.community.officedepot.com/top20list.asp, accessed 9/23/08.
10. www.greendotcompliance.eu/en/packaging-waste-directive-94-62-ec.php, accessed 9/23/08; www.pro-e.org/files/Europe_goes_Green_Dot.pdf, accessed 9/23/08.

11. www.usgbc.org, accessed 9/23/08.

12. U.S. Green Building Council, 2002, *LEED Green Building Rating System, Version 2.1*; available at www.usgbc.org/docs/LEED docs/LEED_RS_v2-1.pdf, accessed 9/23/08.

13. www.usgbc.org, accessed 9/23/08.

14. https://www.climatecare.org/business/business-co2-calculator, accessed 9/23/08.

15. Practical measurement calculations are available in Samantha Putt del Pino and Pankaj Bhatia, *Working 9 to 5 on Climate Change: An Office Guide* (Washington, D.C.: World Resources Institute, 2002), available at: http://pdf.wri.org/wri_co2guide.pdf, accessed 9/23/08.

16. http://sustainability.baxter.com/EHS/2007_environmental_financial_statement.html, accessed 9/23/08.

17. www.globalreporting.org, accessed 9/23/08.

CHAPTER 12

Community Outreach and Respect

After reading this chapter, you will be able to:

- Articulate the competitive advantages of community involvement
- Develop a diverse portfolio of giving opportunities—money, products or services, skills, and job opportunities
- Align community outreach with the company's mission and assets
- Choose community organizations for strategic partnerships
- Administer the community involvement process
- Assess and report social performance

No organization is an island. The well-being of the host community profoundly impacts an organization, and vice versa. Organizations benefit from community development and are disadvantaged by community decay. Organizations can contribute to community well-being, or be an obstacle.

An ethical organization aspires to be a model citizen, joining other stakeholders in creating vibrant communities for the well-being of its employees and other residents. It is in the company's self-interest to do so.

In developing a community giving program, managers must determine the business case for community involvement, what to give, whom to give to and how to manage the community involvement process, and what community impacts to assess and report. This chapter examines each of these issues.

Business Case for Community Involvement

There are an infinite number of daily business problems demanding the attention of managers. Why not save your resources by letting other businesses bear the extra burden of improving community well-being while your organization receives the benefits?

A very strong business case supports being a model citizen. All the competitive advantages of ethical organizations discussed in Chapter 1 apply to community involvement. A company's reputation as a good citizen favorably impacts customer, employee, and governmental relations.

The benefits of active community outreach to the company include:[1]

Benefits to Customer Relations

- Increased brand awareness and recognition
- Customer loyalty

- New business opportunities from collaborating with other involved companies
- First-mover advantages

Benefits to Employee Relations

- Attracting and retaining employees
- A more productive and healthier workforce
- Employees develop a deeper sense of purpose and mission

Benefits to Community Relations

- Preferences with local banks
- Recognition as a responsible neighbor of choice
- Community goodwill and support

The millennial generation, people born between 1980 and 2000, are a key constituent in many long-range business plans. They are replacing the mass outmigration of baby boomers in employment and consumer markets. Among the millennial generation, a company's philanthropic reputation and community involvement is a very important selling point to job seekers and consumers.[2]

Companies can use all the positive marketing help they can get to increase consumer awareness. A wide range of people and organizations seeking to create a better world advertise the products and services of socially responsible organizations. *The Good Shopping Guide*, for instance, highlights companies that respect the environment, animals, and people.[3]

Responding to social trends also helps companies gain first-mover advantages. Wendy's, for instance, was the first fast-food chain to ban unhealthy trans fats from its product. The company was a step ahead of the competition when New York City passed a law banning trans fats from restaurants.[4] Companies already acting in a socially responsible manner are often invited to participate in crafting regulations.

A socially irresponsible reputation can be very costly. For many years, Wal-Mart seemed oblivious to the negative publicity it received regarding low wages and insufficient employee benefits. A consulting company found that 8% of their customers had stopped shopping at Wal-Mart because of its bad reputation.[5] Another consulting firm determined that if Wal-Mart's reputation had been equivalent to that of Target, its stock price would have been 8.4% higher.[6]

Investors are paying greater attention to a company's social performance. In December 2004, Southeast Asia was devastated by a tsunami tidal wave. Researchers report that companies donating money to the relief efforts experienced a positive five-day cumulative abnormal stock price return following their press releases.[7]

What to Give

What do nonprofit organizations and the community need from businesses? Four things:

1. Money
2. Products or services
3. Skills
4. Job opportunities

A systematic giving program would cover all four areas. Giving money and products or services are very meaningful ways to contribute that require minimal time and effort. Giving skills and job opportunities require significantly more time and effort.

Salesforce.com, which provides on-demand customer relationship management services, applies a "1/1/1 Model" for giving money, products, and skills: 1% of new shares of stock are placed in the company foundation for philanthropic purposes, 1% of the company's products are donated to nonprofit organizations, and 1% of employee working hours (four hours a month, or six days annually) are allocated to community service.[8] The company foundation provides grants to any nonprofit organization where a community action team, composed of at least four company employees, volunteers at least 25 hours.

Giving Money

Many nonprofit organizations operate with minimal financial resources and depend on philanthropic donations to serve clients. According to the Giving USA Foundation, corporations donated $12 billion in 2004.[9] Monetary donations can range from putting money in the Salvation Army kettle to the Bill and Melinda Gates Foundation donating $35 billion to address social problems worldwide.

Some companies link the sales of particular products to their philanthropic contributions. Cause-related marketing took off during the 1980s, when American Express donated a penny to the Statue of Liberty restoration project each time a consumer used the company's credit card. Ben & Jerry's upped the ante, donating 1% of the profits from its Peace Pop ice cream novelty bar to peace organizations.

In 2006, Bono, the U2 rock group singer and activist, and Bobby Shriver launched (RED). A portion of profits for all licensed (RED) products are donated to the Global Fund, which finances AIDS programs focused on women and children in Africa.[10] None of the (RED) money can be used to pay overhead expenses. Early corporate partners include Converse, Gap, Motorola, Apple, Hallmark, and Dell.

Giving Products or Services

Many community organizations can benefit from receiving company products or supplies. A low-income community center would be happy to receive school supplies from retail stores, food from grocery stores, books from publishers, and so on.

Timberland, which makes boots, shoes, clothes, and gear for the outdoors, has an extensive product donation program.[11] The company proactively solicits product donation requests from organizations connected with the company's mission, such as environmental volunteer programs. Footwear samples and other product donations benefit underprivileged youth and homeless shelters. Timberland also encourages nonprofits to leverage their product donations as fundraising auction items.

TIPS AND TECHNIQUES

A Highly Integrated Win-Win Donation

Mattel's American Girl division, formerly the Pleasant Company, created a win-win opportunity for the environment, a nonprofit organization, children, and itself. The unique partnership integrates product donations, volunteers, and philanthropy.[12]

Rather than disposing product returns into a landfill, the company donates returned American Girl dolls to the Madison Children's Museum, which then recruits volunteers to repair the dolls. The repaired dolls are resold, at discounted prices, during an annual benefit sale. The proceeds fund Madison Children's Museum programs and other children organizations.

This arrangement expands the American Girl customer base. The discounted prices make the dolls more affordable to a wider range of consumers.

Giving Skills

In 2005, 65.4 million Americans over the age of 16 volunteered—approximately 29% of the adult population.[13] Companies can tap into an employee's desire to help others by supporting volunteer activities and offering sabbaticals.

Some companies set aside one day a year for all employees to serve the community. In a small company, all employees usually work on the same project, such as working together on a Habitat for Humanity project or painting for nonprofits or the elderly, and use the activity as an opportunity for team building and networking. Larger companies typically provide a menu of community involvement opportunities, and employees or departments choose the activity they find most interesting.

The United Way sponsors a "Day of Caring" in many communities and creates projects with nonprofit organizations that make it easy for company employees to participate. Some companies develop their own database of volunteer opportunities. PNC Financial Services Group provides employees with contacts at 200 nonprofits nationwide.[14]

The United Way also recruits business leaders and mid-level managers to sit on the boards of nonprofit organizations. The United Way's computerized system collects data about an employee's skill set and then matches the potential volunteer to the needs of nonprofits. Accountants, for instance, can perform bookkeeping duties, marketing employees design communication materials, and information technology specialists update computer systems.

Wal-Mart's volunteerism in response to the Hurricane Katrina catastrophe in New Orleans is particularly noteworthy.[15] In addition to quickly pledging $15 million to the disaster relief fund and donating more than $3 million in products, the company applied its supply chain management skills and expertise in transportation logistics to coordinate the delivery of merchandise to emergency relief organizations. The resultant positive media coverage contributed to changing Wal-Mart's previously negative reputation.

A growing number of companies offer employees short- or long-term sabbaticals, or leave programs, for community involvement activities.[16] Sabbaticals are a retention policy that appeals to people who are in high-stress jobs, on the verge of burnout, travel a great deal, are looking for new challenges to apply and develop their skills, or simply want to give back to the community. The sabbatical-bound employee should train a replacement, which provides the company an excellent opportunity to develop another high-potential employee.

Some companies also use sabbaticals during economic downturns as an alternative to laying off a highly skilled employee whose job task is temporarily not needed.

Employee sabbaticals should be linked with the employee's skills and career goals. Direct benefits to the employee include improving leadership and project management skills, obtaining a broad perspective of the local community, and gaining new community contacts. At the international level, Pfizer offers volunteer opportunities in developing nations to give employees a firsthand experience with economic development and political dynamics.

Key issues to consider when creating a sabbatical program include:

Who qualifies. Will the employee be chosen based on years of employment, performance achievements, or some other criterion?

For how long. Will the sabbatical be for one week, three weeks, two months, a year?

Where. Will the activity be performed locally, nationally, or internationally?

Type of Activity. Will the activity be community service, small-business assistance, travel immersion, writing a book, or anything?

Compensation. Will the employee receive full pay, reduced pay, or no pay?

Post-Sabbatical Obligation. Does the employee have to remain with the company for a certain period of time after the sabbatical?

Giving Job Opportunities

In addition to giving money, products, and skills, businesses can give back to the community by providing jobs to people in need. One of the most important aspects of a person's life is having a job. Applying a skill for the benefit of an organization contributes to the development of a meaningful life. People tend to take this for granted until they are without a job.

Soon after Hurricane Katrina hit the Gulf Coast in 2005, Wal-Mart promised a job for every one of its displaced workers. Wal-Mart could have simply laid them off due to the natural disaster, but didn't.

Companies can also create special job positions for people with disabilities, the elderly, and returning war veterans. Some nonprofit organizations train people with mental or physical disabilities to re-enter the workforce. Job coaches assist them at the workplace and, when needed, fill in for them if the person with disabilities is unable to work a particular day.

A group of people most in need of job opportunities are ex-convicts. Many prisons offer vocational training, and prisoners can earn technical and advanced degrees while serving time. But recidivism rates remain high because, once released from jail, the ex-convict is unable to obtain employment and falls back to criminal behaviors to earn income.

The government encourages the employment of former prisoners. Companies can receive a federal tax credit of up to $2,400 the first year employing a formerly incarcerated person. Companies can also apply for government-provided insurance to protect against theft by a recently hired ex-convict.

Giving to Whom?

Small business owners operating on Main Street and corporate foundation officers secluded in headquarters are both inundated with requests for assistance.

Managers can reactively give on a first-come first-serve basis, outsource giving to the United Way and other mediating organizations, or proactively give and develop a few key strategic partnerships with nonprofit organizations. Companies should pursue an integrative approach that involves all three types of recipients.

Reactive Giving

Companies should set aside some of their community giving resources to support local nonprofit organizations and causes that are meaningful to employees and community members. These organizations may have unforeseen emergencies or just haphazardly request assistance.

For instance, due to an unanticipated sudden budget shortfall the public high school's theater program might find itself on the verge of being eliminated. A company can have a tremendous impact and gain favorable local publicity by meeting this emergency need. Employee goodwill is generated if several employees have children who benefit from the program. Supporting community organizations that directly impact employees enhances morale and company pride.

Other times, a national emergency, such as Hurricane Katrina, may create a need for immediate assistance. Involving employees in developing a company response to these emergencies unites them on a high profile common cause. The goodwill it generates can spill over into everyday work relationships.

Companies must ensure that their charitable donations do the most good and actually benefit the intended recipients. The American Institute of Philanthropy (AIP) *Charity Rating Guide & Watchdog*

Report grades more than 500 national charities based on how non-profits spend their donations.[17] A list of the top-rated charities is available on AIP's Web site.[18]

Attributes of the top-rated charities are:

- Spends more than 75% of their budgets on programs
- Spends no more than $25 to raise $100 in public support
- Does not hold excessive assets in reserve
- Discloses financial information and documents to AIP

Charity Navigator, an independent nonprofit organization, rates the financial health of more than 5,000 charities in terms of daily operations and program sustainability.[19]

The organization recommends that companies answer the following six questions before donating money to a particular charity:

1. Can the charity clearly communicate who they are and what they do?
2. Can the charity define its short-term and long-term goals?
3. Does the charity report progress made toward its goals?
4. Are the charity's programs rational and productive?
5. Can you trust the charity?
6. Are you willing to make a long-term commitment to the charity?

Outsourcing Giving

Companies should set aside some of their community giving resources to support the local United Way or some other highly credible organization that monitors the disbursement of donations.

The United Way was created as an efficient method for businesses to pool their resources for the benefit of community nonprofit organizations. The United Way performs community needs assessments and ensures that nonprofit recipients appropriately manage donations. The United Way is strongly supported by many local government officials and is an important business networking opportunity.

International outsourcing organizations such as GlobalGiving provide donors with a broad range of social projects to fund; those such as Kiva provide a broad range of individual recipients to fund. These organizations take responsibility for screening recipients and holding them accountable.

GlobalGiving,[20] created in 2002 by former World Bank executives, links donors to specific projects. A company's community outreach committee can browse the GlobalGiving Web site and research causes either by topic (e.g., children, environment) or location. The recipient organizations are legally accountable to GlobalGiving for meeting standardized compliance measures.

GlobalGiving ensures that 85–90% of the tax-deductible donation is put to use by the recipient organization within 60 days. Donors are given quarterly updates from the recipient organization about the project's progress. GlobalGiving offers donors a satisfaction guarantee of up to $10,000. If not pleased with the project's progress, the donor can request a voucher for the original donation amount and reallocate the money to a different project.

Kiva, founded in 2005, is a person-to-person microloan lending Web site that links donors/lenders to entrepreneurs in underdeveloped or developing nations who are unable to obtain loans from regular banking institutions.[21] Technically, this is not a donation, because the money is being loaned to the recipient with the intent of repayment. The donor browses entrepreneur profiles, selects one, and sends the money to Kiva, which deposits the money with a nearby microfinance institution. The microfinance institution also offers the entrepreneur training and other assistance. After the entrepreneur pays back the loan, the donor can reissue another loan to the entrepreneur, lend the money to a different entrepreneur, or withdraw the funds.

Proactive Giving and Strategic Philanthropy

Companies should also set aside some community giving resources for strategic partnerships with nonprofits aligned with the company's mission.

The strategic partnership could be based on what community organization benefits the most by aligning with the company or benefits the company the most. The ideal strategic partner is an organization at the intersection of these approaches, where both the company and the organization receive optimal benefits.

Scholastic Books, for instance, funds literacy programs. Klinke Cleaners collects coats for kids during the winter holiday season. Nabisco produced a series of Animal Crackers in the shape of endangered species and donated product sales to the World Wildlife Fund. The donation recipients are also potential customers.

Exhibit 12.1 provides questions managers should ask to help them determine which community organizations can benefit the most by being aligned with the company.

EXHIBIT 12.1

Community Organizations that Benefit the Most from a Strategic Partnership

Determine a nonprofit strategic partner by answering the following questions:

1. *Mission Match*
   a. What is your company's mission?
   b. What community organizations have a mission that intersects this mission?

2. *Product or Service Match*
   a. What is your company's product or service?
   b. What community organizations would benefit from this product or service?

3. *Employee Skills Match*
   a. What skills can your employees offer a community organization?
   b. What community organizations would benefit from these skills?

An optimal partner is a community organization with a similar mission that can benefit from the company's product, service, and employee skills.

The company should also explore strategic partnerships with community organizations that supply inputs to the company or purchase the company's outputs.

Companies, for instance, need high-quality laborers. Donating money, products, or skills to educational institutions that develop future employees enhances a company's competitive advantage. Similarly, a company that wants to expand its customer base should donate to organizations whose managers or employees are associated with key target markets. A retail jewelry store, for instance, should donate money, product, and skills to a nonprofit organization whose members, or service recipients, fit the company's customer profile.

Sometimes the input supplier and potential customer base overlap. These organizations are very attractive strategic partners. By donating computers to educational institutions, Dell develops the labor skills of potential future employees and creates a future customer base among the student population.

Exhibit 12.2 provides questions managers should ask to help them determine which community organizations can contribute the most to the company achieving its strategic goals.[22]

EXHIBIT 12.2

Community Organizations that Benefit the Company the Most

Partnership Factor	Probing Questions: What community organizations . . .
Sources of Potential Employees or Other Resources	• Have similar labor and product supply chains? • Train and develop potential employees? • Attract high-quality potential employees to the community? • Serve as incubators for research and development ideas? • Develop and protect necessary natural resources?

	• Are associated with current and potential sources of capital? • Attract potential suppliers to the community? • Can contribute to cost reductions? • Have similar infrastructure needs?
Sources of Potential Customers	• Currently, or could, purchase products or services? • Serve current and potential customers? • Make the location a more attractive place for potential customers? • Stimulate business development and economic growth?

A community organization that rises to the top after applying the questions in Exhibit 12.1 (community organizations that benefit the most) and Exhibit 12.2 (community organizations that benefit the company the most) is an optimal choice for a win-win strategic partnership.

The ideal partnership is an equal partnership. Company managers must be empathetic to the problems of managing community organizations and vice versa. Businesses must acknowledge and honor the community organization's limitations, and work within those limits to develop quality win-win projects. Strategic partnership objectives must be transparent, fair, and realistic, with two-way communication between community organization and business.

Team Building and Project Management Training Opportunities

Community involvement provides an opportunity for team building, leadership training, and teaching project management, all of which directly impact a company's daily operations. Go-getters, in particular, need diverse opportunities to use their creativity, develop talents, and hone managerial skills.

Volunteering on a common cause benefitting the community enhances employee morale. Workplace relationships can get monotonous and frayed over time. Employee interactions while serving food at a homeless shelter or building a Habitat for Humanity home, for instance, create common experiences that keep relationships fresh and meaningful.

Timberland uses community service projects to teach employees project management skills. The employee leading the project defines its scope, researches community needs and assets, selects the service partner, develops the project, prepares a budget and plan, motivates participants, manages the event, measures outcomes, and celebrates the accomplishments.[23] The company provides the team leader with tools and worksheets to enable successful completion of the project.

Community Involvement Management Process

Determining what to give which organization could be determined by the human resources office, a philanthropic foundation, or a team of employees. Even if a company is large enough to support its own foundation, employees should be involved in the outreach decision-making process.

The process for authentic engagement between the company and community closely parallels "Managing Environmental Change" in Exhibit 11.3. Exhibit 12.3 expands on that model.

EXHIBIT 12.3

Community Involvement Management Process

Step	Action	Explanation
1.	Assign a community involvement champion	This is an opportunity to provide leadership training to a go-getter at the middle management or nonmanagement level.
2.	Obtain management support	Executives should provide visible and vocal support for the program.
3.	Form a community involvement team	A cross-functional employee team can obtain participation throughout the company.
4.	Conduct a company asset analysis	Determine the amount or type of money, time, product, and skills the company can contribute.
5.	Gather information on community needs	Obtain information from the employees and the United Way.
6.	Match *company* assets and *community* needs	Determine potential links between company assets and community needs and prioritize these win-win possibilities.
7.	Match *community* assets and *company* needs	Determine potential links between community assets and company needs and prioritize these win-win possibilities.

(Continued)

EXHIBIT 12.3

(Continued)		
Step	**Action**	**Explanation**
8.	Develop a strategic partnership with a community organization	Form a strategic alliance with a community partner, gather suggestions on the type of assistance they need most, and reach agreement on an action plan.
9.	Create a vision and goal statement	In partnership with the community organization, create an overall vision statement and several goals for the highest priority items.
10.	Determine a practical application	Focus on "low-hanging fruit" where the company's involvement can make a difference or a high-profile issue employees strongly support.
11.	Involve other employees in the community involvement process	Share the vision and goal with other employees and provide outlets for employee input.
12.	Assess performance	Develop measures to assess performance, gather other relevant feedback for continuous improvement, and make changes as needed.
13.	Support other opportunities	Provide flexibility for employees to take responsibility for other community involvement initiatives.

Community Reputation Assessment

The Council on Foundations has created a Corporate Philanthropy Index (CPI) for companies to assess their reputation within the community. The three-item survey, measured on a one-to-five Likert scale, should be sent to multiple stakeholders or administered at a focus group meeting.[24] The survey items are:

- Compared to other companies, (Company Name) does its fair share to help the community and society.

- Overall, (Company Name) is the kind of company that helps the community and society by contributing things like time, volunteers, money, and sponsorships of nonprofit events and causes.

- (Company Name) really seems to care about giving and making contributions to help the community and society.

Social Performance Reporting

A company can also demonstrate respect for the community by being transparent about its operations and impacts. The Global Reporting Initiative (GRI) discussed in Chapter 11 offers a standardized framework for community impact reporting, in addition to environmental performance.[25] GRI examined 72 sustainability reports and found that most companies reported community impacts in the areas of education and training, philanthropy and charitable giving, community services and employee volunteering, total community expenditure, and community engagement and dialogue.

The top three indicators used to measure performance in each of the five areas appear in Exhibit 12.4.[26] Adopting this format enables companies to make comparisons with other firms in their region or industry.

EXHIBIT 12.4

Top Three Indicators for Five Community Impact Topics

Education and Training

1. Number of people benefited/reached by education initiatives
2. Amount of money invested/donated in the education initiatives
3. Number of education-related activities (e.g., seminars, classes, conferences, etc.) held

Philanthropy and Charitable Giving

1. Sum of money donated/raised/contributed to community initiatives
2. Percentage or number of people (organizations) granted/sponsored/covered by donated services
3. Number of quantity of scholarships/materials/services donated

Community Services and Employee Volunteering

1. Number of people/organizations/projects benefited, served, or implemented
2. Number of volunteers
3. Number of volunteering hours

Total Community Expenditure

1. Amount of money spent in community investment
2. Percentage of profit/revenue/income spent
3. Percentage increase of money spent on social investment, compared to last year

4. Number of people benefited through community investment activities

5. Number of projects developed and completed

Community Engagement and Dialogue

1. Number of visitors, audience, and participants reached

2. Percentage/number of sites where community engagement activities were performed

3. Frequency of meetings

Ben & Jerry's,[27] Timberland,[28] and Starbucks,[29] three leading companies in the area of social reporting, publicize their community involvement reports on the Internet and offer them as models for other companies to adapt.

Summary

Companies possess tremendous amounts of power in their host communities. They can contribute to community well-being or decay. Nonprofit organizations, which usually arise because of market failures, depend on the generosity of companies to serve their clients.

This chapter recommends a diverse approach to community outreach. Companies should give money, products and services, skills, and job opportunities to the community. Companies should also give to community organizations that are supported by employees, outsource giving to organizations that carefully monitor how community organizations use donations, and develop strategic partnerships with community organizations that are aligned with the company's strategic goals and objectives.

Community outreach provides an opportunity for companies to conduct team-building exercises, train future managers in project management, and provide leadership opportunities to go-getters. The community involvement process must be carefully measured and the outcomes assessed and shared with the community.

Community outreach, a hallmark of ethical organizations, is a win-win opportunity for companies, nonprofit organizations, and the host community. The relationship must be based on respect, fairness, and transparency.

As demonstrated by *In the Real World: Arthur Andersen's Document/ Retention Policy—October 2001*, respect, fairness, and transparency were not prominent values in the network of relationships among Enron, Arthur Andersen, and the SEC. This contributed to the collapse of two high-profile companies—Enron and Arthur Andersen. Both of these businesses were considered, at one time, ethical role models in their respective industries.

IN THE REAL WORLD

Arthur Andersen's Document Retention Policy—October 2001

On October 16, 2001, Ken Lay violated federal law by lying to shareholders. He announced that Enron had third-quarter operating losses of $618 million and $1.01 billion in nonrecurring write-offs. He failed to report an additional $5 billion in hidden losses. The nonrecurring write-offs attracted public attention. The SEC began an "informal" investigation, and the *Wall Street Journal*'s investigative journalists began publishing articles describing how CFO Andy Fastow profited from managing SPEs that did business with Enron.

Arthur Andersen found itself in a bind. Andersen was already under a cease–and–desist order from the SEC for its role in an accounting fraud at Waste Management, the giant trash-removal firm. The SEC threatened to disbar Andersen from practicing public accounting if it did not cease and desist from other fraudulent activities. Now it was becoming obvious that, a mere four months later, Andersen had been fraudulently certifying the books of another client—Enron.

Nancy Temple, Andersen's in-house lawyer, was among those creating a paper trail documenting Andersen's concerns about the Enron audit. Four days prior to Lay's October 16 financial statement announcement, Temple sent an e-mail to Andersen's Houston office reminding them about Andersen's "documentation retention and destruction policy."

According to the policy, all nonessential audit materials could be destroyed prior to the initiation of a formal SEC investigation. Nothing could be destroyed after the SEC announced a formal investigation. The e-mail was forwarded to David Duncan, the lead auditor on the Enron account, for his consideration.

Duncan's engagement team had been very lax. The team failed to remove redundant and nonessential documents after completing its two most recent quarterly audits. A formal SEC investigation seemed imminent, but it had not yet been declared. Duncan still had the legal right to destroy redundant and nonessential documents.

DECISION CHOICE. If you were the lead external auditor engagement partner, would you:

 Implement Andersen's document retention and destruction policy and destroy redundant and nonessential documents?

❷ Preserve all Enron documents to assist any future SEC investigation?

Why?

Notes

1. www.cof.org, accessed 9/25/08.

2. Sarah E. Needleman, "The Latest Office Perk," *Wall Street Journal*, April 29, 2008.

3. *The Good Shopping Guide* (London: The Ethical Company Organization, 2006).

4. Pete Engardio, "Beyond the Green Corporation," *Business Week*, January 29, 2007.

5. Marc Gunther, "The Green Machine," *Fortune*, July 27, 2006.

6. Pete Engardio, "Beyond the Green Corporation," *Business Week*, January 29, 2007.

7. Dennis M. Patten, "Does the Market Value Corporate Philanthropy? Evidence from the response to the 2004 Tsunami Relief Effort," *Journal of Business Ethics*, 81, no. 3 (2008): 599-607.

8. www.salesforcefoundation.org/sharethemodel, accessed 9/25/08.

9. Walter W. Powell and Richard Steinberg (eds.), *The Non-Profit Sector*, 2nd edition (New Haven, CT: Yale University Press, 2006): 182.

10. www.joinred.com, accessed 9/25/08.

11. www.timberland.com/corp/index.jsp?page=donationProgram, accessed 9/25/08.

12. Denis Collins and Lisa Goldthorpe, "Smart Seconds," *Madison Magazine*, February 2007: 32-33.

13. See "Volunteering in America: State Trends and Ranking, 2002–2005," www.cns.gov/pdf/VIA/VIA_summaryreport.pdf, accessed 9/25/08.

14. Sarah E. Needleman, "The Latest Office Perk," *Wall Street Journal*, April 29, 2008.

15. Michael Barbaro and Justin Gillis, "Wal-Mart at Forefront of Hurricane Relief," *Washington Post*, September 5, 2005.

16. Andrew E. Carr and Thomas Li-Ping Tang, "Sabbaticals and Employee Motivation: Benefits, Concerns, and Implications," *Journal of Education for Business*, 80, no. 3 (2005): 160-164.

17. www.charitywatch.org, accessed 9/25/08.

18. www.charitywatch.org/toprated.html, accessed 9/25/08.

19. www.charitynavigator.org, accessed 9/25/08.

20. www.globalgiving.com, accessed 9/25/08.

21. www.kiva.org, accessed 9/25/08.

22. Michael E. Porter and Mark R. Kramer, 2002, "The Competitive Advantage of Corporate Philanthropy," *Harvard Business Review*, 80, no. 12 (2002): 56-68.

23. www.timberland.com/corp/TimberlandServiceToolKit.pdf, accessed 9/25/08.

24. www.cof.org/members/content.cfm?itemnumber=761&navItem Number=2409, accessed 9/25/08.

25. www.globalreporting.org/ReportingFramework/G3Guidelines, accessed 9/25/08.

26. Global Reporting Initiative, 2008, "Reporting on Community Impacts," available at www.globalreporting.org/NR/rdonlyres/ 6D00BC14-2035-42AB-AB6A-5102F1FF8961/0/CIReportfi nalnew.pdf, 11, accessed 9/25/08.

27. www.benjerry.com/our_company/about_us/social_mission/social _audits/2006_sear, accessed 9/25/08.

28. www.timberland.com/corp/index.jsp?page=./include/csr_reports, accessed 9/25/08.

29. Starbucks Corporation Corporate Social Responsibility Fiscal 2007 Annual Report, available at: www.starbucks.com/aboutus/csrreport/Coffee_Report_PDF_FY07.pdf, accessed 9/25/08.

Index